CW00585146

Attacking the Devil:

130 Years of
The Northern Echo

Chris Lloyd

What a glorious opportunity of attacking the devil is n't it?

Foreword by Harold Evans

First published in December 1999 by *The Northern Echo*, Priestgate, Darlington, Co Durham DL1 1NF. *The Northern Echo* is part of Newsquest (North East) Ltd which is a Gannett company

www.thisisthenortheast

Text copyright © *The Northern Echo* 1999

British Library Cataloguing in Publication Data
A catalogue record for this book is available from the British Library

ISBN 1-899432-14-0

Printed by Gordian Print Ltd of Middlesbrough
Bound by John Joyce and Son of Gateshead

Cover picture: **The Northern Echo's** *headquarters in Priestgate, Darlington, in January 1952 and November 1999*

Contents

Introduction

WHY? As a southerner settling in the North-East of England and forging a modest career on the Great Daily of the North with its proud, almost fearsome, reputation of campaigning and caring for its community, *why?* was a question that bothered me.

The Northern Echo was first printed on January 1, 1870, and the accepted explanations for its existence involve railways and well-intentioned Liberals. But they alone can't fully answer the question *why?* because a local weekly, perhaps with regional pretensions, would have been a sufficient response to them. The sudden advent of a giant of a regional morning with a voice that could be heard attacking the devil all over the country – even across the Continent – is just too much for those explanations to bear.

For most of its first 130 years, *The Northern Echo* has been unique among newspapers: its circulation has been bigger than the population of the town, Darlington, in which it is based.

And for all of its first 59 years, *The Northern Echo* seems not to have made a halfpenny profit. The question *why?* elicits no more than a shake of the head and the passing thought that the paper really shouldn't exist at all... Until you delve deeper and discover a frighteningly close shave with unthinkable embarrassment which acted as an almighty kick up the bottom for the local Establishment. That kick came from a marvellous maverick, who has become one of my historic heroes, and it propelled *The Northern Echo* into existence.

But that only answers the beginning bit of *why?* Once alive, *The Northern Echo* quickly gathered a formidable reputation – a reputation best summed up by WT Stead's phrase "attacking the devil" – and around it grew a nationwide empire of newspapers.

More questions crowd in. How, not once but twice, did *The Northern Echo* suddenly find new lease of life when it appeared to be a declining relic from a bygone age. And finally, just as the dinosaurs were hit by some unexplained calamity, what struck *The Northern Echo* and made its circulation decline catastrophically? And *why?*, then, does it still exist so successfully, still attacking the devil with vigour after 130 years, at the dawn of the 21st Century.

So the reason for this book is *why?*, and I believe that it answers my original question and many more besides about the Great Daily of the North.

Chris Lloyd
Priestgate, November 1999

Foreword

I AM honoured to light this impressive candle on the 130th anniversary of *The Northern Echo*. The newspaper, which I regard as the heart of the North-East region, has had an extraordinary history since John Hyslop Bell launched it as the first halfpenny daily in England.

Of course, its most famous editor, W.T. Stead, was a Northumberland man and his contribution to journalism merits a fireworks show of its own. It was from Darlington that he launched the great campaign against Turkish atrocities in Bulgaria, which Gladstone applauded, before leaving for London and the Maiden Tribute of Modern Babylon, the exposure of the white slave traffic for which he went to jail. Stead proved that Darlington was a fine place from which to view the world, and agitate for change, and *The Northern Echo* came to speak for the region.

Many people must be acknowledged in that long-sustained success story – enlightened ownership ready to invest in good journalism and defend editorial independence; the craftsmen in the hot metal composing room and pressroom; redoubtable reporters and photographers; advertising men and managers; and a good run of editors, many who served for decades.

In my time in the 1960s, Westminster Press was supportive of all our efforts to make the North-East a better place to live and work – and to educate the heathen south of York.

My experiences in America with the current ownership, Gannett, give me confidence that they will maintain the best traditions of *The Northern Echo*.

Of course, the many achievements of the paper over 130 years would not have been possible without the loyalty of the readers to "The Echo". We all have something to celebrate today.

Harold M. Evans

Vice Chairman & Editorial Director
U.S. News & World Report/Daily News/The Atlantic Monthly/Fast Company
New York
October 1999

1 Dawning of the newspaper era

NEWSPAPERS were a nuisance. They were troublesome little rags that were forever stirring their readers into rebellion. They cared little for truth but preferred to foment agitation.

And so the rulers of Georgian and early Victorian Britain did their best to ensure that the working man should never get his dirty hands on an inky paper. They slapped taxes on every conceivable aspect of a newspaper: on the paper on which it was printed, on the advertisements it carried to subsidise its subversive publication and, just for good measure, on the newspaper itself. Of a cover price of 5d, 3½d was taxes.

As well as making newspapers prohibitively expensive, these taxes prevented new publications from entering the market dominated by The Times, the Government's mouthpiece. The taxes were levied at a flat rate so that a well-established newspaper with a large circulation – say The Times – paid as much as a newly-founded paper with a tiny circulation in the provinces – say, Darlington.

The taxes were usually increased during times of war. This both swelled the Government's war coffers and prevented families from buying a paper and discovering the fate of loved ones fighting on foreign fields. It is little coincidence that the very beginnings of the popular newspaper era can be traced to the time of the Crimean War of 1855 when the public was demanding information about what was being done in its name to its sons.

In the 1840s and 1850s there was a concerted campaign against these "taxes on knowledge" very similar in tone to that fought by newspapers, including *The Northern Echo*, over 130 years later against the threat of the imposition of Value Added Tax. Back then, it was also pointed out that the taxes were actually encouraging the spread of unfounded gossip because printers would publish scurrilous sheets, stir up trouble and move on before the Revenue came calling.

Indeed, it was the Revenue which closed the very first newspaper – or should that be pamphlet? – to be published in Darlington. This newspaper – sorry, pamphlet – was called The Darlington Pamphlet, Or County of Durham Intelligencer. It first appeared on May 22, 1772 and cost just 2d. This was because its printer, J Sadler, thought that by calling his publication a pamphlet as opposed to a newspaper, he would be able to wriggle untaxed through a loophole.

Sadly, Sadler was unsuccessful. The Revenue rumbled the ruse. The last edition appeared on November 20 of the same year and was given away free.

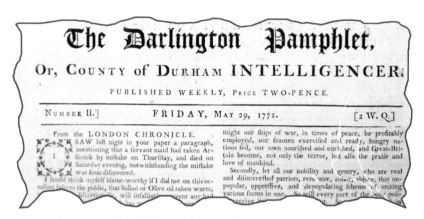

The Darlington Pamphlet of 1772, Darlington's first newspaper

Sorrowfully, Sadler wrote his farewell in a single sentence of epic proportions: "Having received orders from the commissioners of the stamp duties to stop publication of this paper under a supposition of its being liable to that duty I am under the necessity of submitting to their injunctions rather than run the risk of trying this undetermined point of law at my own expense when I consider 'tis waging war with the mint, yet notwithstanding this I have laid my case before some eminent counsel in London and hope to receive their opinion very soon, which if in my favour under that sanction, the pamphlet will be again revived and published as usual, but, on the contrary, if I should be obliged to print it on a sheet of stamped paper I hope my customers will not think the addition of an half penny a week too much as it will be one penny per week more to me and I take the opportunity of returning my most sincere thanks to all subscribers and to request the continuance of their favours which will be ever gratefully acknowledged by their obliged humble servant J Sadler, Darlington, November 1772."

The Darlington Pamphlet, Or County Durham Intelligencer never reappeared – although Sadler did the following year with the equally short-lived Darlington Mercury. However, it may not solely have been the Revenue that did for the Pamphlet. Most of the advertisements in the paper were for patent medicines like Ague Powders, Astmatic Pills and Balsam of Liquorice. The wholesaler in Darlington of these cures was none other than Mr J Sadler, who was also the official printer for the town's Chief Bailiff. The distributors of the Pamphlet were all sub-agents for Saddler, selling on his medicinal compounds. Perhaps the Pamphlet failed because sensible Darlingtonians tired of the quack remedies they were being force fed by the printer.

Darlington's first penny daily, The Northern Daily Express, quickly moved to Newcastle

It wasn't until 1853 that the authorities began changing their attitude towards newspapers and removed the advertising duty. The paper tax was repealed in 1861, but the most important reform of all was the removal of the heaviest duty of all, the newspaper stamp tax, in June 1855.

This heralded the era of the "penny dailies". In Darlington, John Watson founded the Northern Daily Express on April 21. When the repeal came in on June 30, he was able to cut his cover price from 2d to 1d, although he quickly discovered that Darlington was not a big enough metropolis to support a daily paper and so on October 30 he switched publication to Newcastle. On a national level, the most famous penny daily to spring from this reform was The Daily Telegraph which first published on September 17, 1855, priced 1d.

Other political changes that assisted the newspaper climate followed apace. Much importance, for example, has been attached to the 1870 Education Act. Known as the Forster Act after its prime mover, this revolutionised elementary education. Previously schools had been run by private individuals or charitable institutions: the Forster Act introduced state schools paid for by rates and taxes.

This undoubtedly gave a greater impetus to the newspaper industry, but if it did make the common man more literate and so more interested in learning about the world around him from newspapers, it cannot have had any beneficial effect on the newspaper market for a decade when those first pupils of the Forster revolution left school.

There is increasing evidence to suggest that before the 1870 Act, between two-thirds and three-quarters of the male population was already able to read – 80 per cent of them signed their marriage certificates with their name as opposed to a mark which suggests at least some degree of literacy.

This, sadly, rather ruins the delightfully romantic vision of hundreds of people, thirsting for knowledge but unable to read it, crowding round Bulmer's Stone in Darlington waiting to drink in every word read aloud from the day's paper by a well educated person standing on the Stone. They are more likely to have been there because they couldn't afford their own heavily-taxed copy – and if they had splashed out, their conditions at home were not conducive to reading such poorly designed efforts. In a two-up, two-down with an outside toilet 50 yards away with ten or 13 children milling around, a miner would have been mad to settle down at the end of a long shift with a newspaper and try to make out the tiny type in dense columns by the light of a flickering candle.

The Sunday papers like the News of the World, on the other hand, were a different prospect: they were a once-a-week expense and the salacious material contained within their compact columns could be read – joy of joys – in daylight hours on the day of rest.

And the reason daily papers weren't designed to entice and encourage casual readership? Reproduction techniques didn't allow early proprietors to use photographs or drawings, but beyond that, the constraints on their design skills were imposed by the dreaded "taxes on knowledge". The newspaper stamp tax was levied on each printed sheet. Early sub-editors, therefore, had to concentrate on cramming as many small words onto a single page as possible. Expansive headlines and elaborate crossheads, which would have enlivened the columns, would have caused the news to spill over onto another heavily-taxed sheet.

In political terms, more relevant to the newspaper industry than the Education Act was probably the 1868 Reform Act which extended the franchise to more of the population. It was followed by an awakening of the workers' rights

Looking north down Northgate, Darlington. Bulmer's Stone has rested here for centuries, poorer people reputedly gathering around it to hear the day's news

movement which within 30 years had led to the formation of the Labour Party. And in those days when the patent for the telephone was still eight years away, when cinema newsreels, radio and television were not even a twinkling in a cathode ray tube, and when the Internet was inconceivable, newspapers were the only medium through which the new voters and workers could obtain information, and the only medium through which the political parties could spread their messages.

Indeed, a year after the Reform Act the John Bull publication remarked of the Conservatives' rout at the polls: "The party lost fearfully at the elections through lack of sufficient newspaper support." *The Northern Echo's* first triumph as a campaigning newspaper would come at the next General Election in 1874, four years after it first appeared, with the "Durham 13" – all 13 of the MPs elected for the county of Durham would be Liberals for the first time in history. The Echo claimed this as a great personal success because in the rest of the country the Liberal vote collapsed spectacularly.

Just as important to the fledgling newspaper industry as the political changes were the great advances in technology. The most obvious, which had Darlington at its heart, was the growth of the railways which by the 1850s were blossoming into a national network. But for the provincial press, the railways were a double-edged sword: they brought news quickly from London ready for publication in, say, Darlington, but equally they brought rival newspapers quickly from London ready for sale in, say, Darlington.

Far more important to the prospects of newspapers removed from London was the advent of the telegraph in the early 1850s. Initially, it was run by three private companies who charged for every message they transmitted and who were more interested in commercial concerns than the social service of the spread of knowledge. The charging system prevented provincial editors from employing their own correspondents to file their own copy. Instead they relied upon the telegraph companies' own digests of Parliamentary and political events, but because the companies had their minds elsewhere, their digests were often unreliable. Although even today copy from Parliamentary correspondents is sometimes not what it should be, the manifest shortcomings of the telegraph companies' offerings was one of the reasons that in 1868 the Manchester Guardian founded the Press Association, an agency which would provide pooled but reliable reports for the provincials. On December 2, 1869 – 30 days before its first publication – *The Northern Echo* signed up to the Press Association, and is still a subscriber 131 years later.

In 1870, the telegraph companies were nationalised and the Post Office was put in charge of domestic telegraphs. A special lower rate was introduced for newspapers and on February 5, the Press Association started its own telegraphic service.

The importance of this nationalisation cannot be overstated in the development of the newspaper industry. The founder of *The Northern Echo*, John Hyslop Bell, said: "Without cheaper telegraphy, I could not have started the Echo."

The speed of the telegraph also helped provincial newspapers overcome the problem that the expanding railways were causing. A paper in the North-East could now receive London, Parliamentary and even international news (the Dover-Calais cable had opened in 1858) by telegraph hours before the London newspapers could reach the North-East on the train.

Another important advance in technology concerned the printing press. Although invented by William Caxton in 1477, it was now moving into the era of mass-production by utilising steam-power. In 1868, The Times perfected the rotary-web press – plates on drums were spun by steam, printing on a continuous roll of paper. This press could churn out 10,500 copies of an eight page newspaper in an hour.

And so, with all these fiscal, political, social and technological factors coming together, dawn broke over "the golden age of the provincial press". In 1854, there had been 289 provincial papers in the country. In 1871, there were 851. At the forefront of this explosion was a newcomer called *The Northern Echo*.

2 The first halfpenny morning

FOR 61 years, *The Northern Echo* unwittingly confused its readers. On May 30, 1906, its front page titlepiece was redesigned to include the statement: "Founded 1869".

It wasn't until April 26, 1967, that the paper changed its front page declaration to read the more historically accurate: "Founded 1870".

The confusion arises because John Hyslop Bell came to Darlington around the middle of 1869 and began preparing for his great publishing venture. He rented an office in a former thread and shoelace factory in Priestgate – it may have been conveniently empty or it may, given Bell's early espousal of telegraphy, have been conveniently located, close to Northgate Post Office. Incoming telegraphs could have been quickly collected by foot although early in his operation a pneumatic tube connected the sub-editors' room with the Post Office and telegrams from London zooped through for immediate attention.

The location in Priestgate has proved long lastingly convenient. In 1908, when the lease on the former thread factory came up for sale, the Echo was able to buy it along with the empty adjoining corner plot of land that ran around into Crown Street. Only in the late 1980s, when the Cornmill shopping centre was being developed around it, did the Echo consider leaving Bell's original site.

John Hyslop Bell, founder of The Northern Echo

From here in late 1869, Bell printed first a prospectus and then three months of print trials of *The Northern Echo*.

The prospectus for the new paper was a declaration of intent for the "new daily newspaper for the North of England".

Much was made of the fact that the paper would sell for $\frac{1}{2}$d – yes, "one halfpenny!!" – and this would become the Echo's first claim to fame. Halfpenny evening newspapers were not uncommon but they largely rehashed the contents of morning papers and sold in a smaller locality; no regional morning paper had yet been successful charging just half-a-penny.

However, this was Bell's founding principle and his decision. He wanted the

The Echo's first office in a former thread and shoelace factory in Priestgate, Darlington. 130 years later, the paper is still published from the same site

paper to be as cheap as possible so it would attract as many readers as possible. "Having regard to the...great and growing eagerness for early information evinced by all classes of the community, the projectors have come to the conclusion that a Halfpenny Morning Newspaper has become a necessity of the times," says the prospectus, "and they claim the honour of having taken the initiative in supplying that want. They are satisfied that the efficient maintenance of such a daily paper is not only eminently desirable, but also very possible; and not only a possibility, but one that may, by the intelligent application of recent improvements in newspaper machinery and management, be made a commercial success."

It could have been commercial suicide, though. For decades to come, the Echo's development was hampered by Bell's selfless decision. A halfpenny paper simply did not generate the income required for investment to develop the product.

Little wonder that some sceptics scoffed at Bell's sentiments. Sir Joseph Cowen, the Newcastle Liberal MP, remarked dismissively: "I don't know what they mean by a halfpenny morning paper." But then, Sir Joseph was proprietor of the Newcastle Daily Chronicle. He was the North-East's leading newspaper baron and pioneer – his Chronicle, which had become a daily in 1858, was the region's leading newspaper, overshadowing its morning rival, the Newcastle Daily Journal, which had converted from weekly in 1861. The halfpenny upstart in Darlington might not have immediately threatened Sir Joseph's dominance – it wasn't until 1903 that the Echo made a serious attempt to take Tyneside – but it did halve the distance between himself and his nearest Liberal morning rival in Leeds.

After trumpeting the price in the prospectus, Bell's second announcement was the paper's name: *The Northern Echo*. It wasn't until the 1960s that the paper decided it needed more oomph and so the definite article at the beginning of its name received a capital T.

It would appear that Bell was inspired to adopt the name "the Echo" by the success of a halfpenny mid-day and evening London paper called The Echo which had been published two years earlier by Henry Cassell (Bell's inspiration for the Echo also came from further afield, from the Petit Journal which served Paris).

Alternatively, it may be that in Darlington alone within the previous 15 years there had been two Mercurys, a Times, a Telegraph and an Express so his choice of name was pretty limited.

As well as all its other attributes, Cassell's Echo was also a Liberal paper and, as Bell announced in his prospectus, *The Northern Echo* was "to supply a want of the age and district, viz, a well-conducted, high-class Daily Newspaper, advocating Advanced Liberal opinions, and published at a price which will bring it within reach of all classes of the people".

For, prime among all of Bell's attributes, was the fact that he was a Liberal. He was invited to Darlington in 1869 by the Pease family who had ruled the town, unchallenged until frighteningly recently, since they had had the foresight to bring the railways to it in 1825. Their style was beneficent, munificent, philanthropic and paternal. They were very much dyed-in-the-wool (they'd started as 18th Century linen merchants) Liberals and needed an organ to espouse their cause.

Allied to the fact that he was a Liberal, Bell was also an experienced newspaperman. He'd been born in Dumfriesshire in about 1833 (he was aged 88 when he died on May 5, 1920) and had left Scotland for London at the age of 18 to become a civil servant. After three years, he'd changed horses and become a Parliamentary and law reporter. He came north at the age of 22 and became a partner in a Sunderland newspaper with John Candlish MP and Henry Pitman – son of the inventor of another journalistic tool, Pitman's shorthand, and interestingly in the first issue of *The Northern Echo* there are several adverts from H Pitman.

In 1855, in the tax repeal days, this Sunderland paper merged with the South Durham and Cleveland Mercury, a Liberal paper, and Bell was its editor and co-proprietor. He was also a Hartlepool town councillor. It was from there, at the Peases' request, that he transferred to Darlington.

As well as being the Peases' hometown, Darlington had several other attributes that would have proved attractive to Bell – and as he was sole proprietor of the paper for 17 years, he would have had to look at all aspects of the concern.

For a start, Darlington was served by no other morning paper. The Northern Express had briefly flirted with it in 1855 before taking itself off to Newcastle when Darlington proved too small to sustain it. But, as the Peases' enterprises had taken off, the population of the market town had expanded rapidly: in 1861, there were 15,789 residents; in 1871, there were 27,729. By 1911, there would be 55,631.

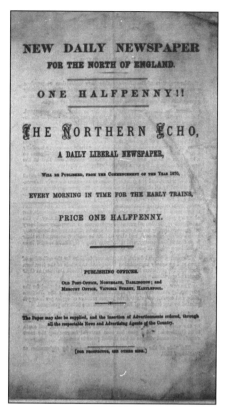

The first page of the three page Prospectus of 1869

And, of course, there were the railways. To other newspapers, the railways were a mixed blessing as they carried competitors' products as well as up-to-date copy. To *The Northern Echo*, the railways were a boon.

Its prospectus states: "A thoroughly organised system will be adopted for the conveyance of the papers by early trains to every station in the North of England, by various lines of railway that radiate east, west, north and south from Darlington; and a plan has been matured for reaching the more remote towns and villages at the earliest possible moment."

Darlington was at the centre of the rail network. As well as laying claim to the title of "the first halfpenny morning", it could also have claimed to be Britain's first true national newspaper. Because of rail distribution, its morning edition was simultaneously on sale in both of the country's great capitals: London and Edinburgh. It took nine hours for the London-based newspapers who laughably called themselves 'nationals' to reach the Scottish capital. By that time their news was stale, thanks to the prompt delivery of *The Northern Echo*.

In 1874, WT Stead was able to boast: "*The Northern Echo* can be had in London and Edinburgh respectively at ten o'clock each morning of publication, and at all intervening railway stations, north and south of Darlington, at a proportionately early hour."

What is more, Darlington in its pre-Echo days was practically crying out for its own newspaper because the town was in danger of being overshadowed by its pre-eminent neighbour to the north, Newcastle. This need had been shown on February 26, 1848, when the country was stunned to learn of the abdication of Louis Philippe in Paris. Francis Mewburn, "the railway solicitor" and diarist, wrote: "Such was the anxiety at Newcastle to have the newspapers that a telegraph despatched from Gateshead station to Darlington ordered all the newspapers to be forwarded to Newcastle." Usually, the London morning papers came north on the train, being dropped off at each station en route from where they were distributed. On this occasion, Newcastle seems to have been so eager to read of the abdication that it commandeered little Darlington's delivery.

Mewburn noted: "The stationmaster at Darlington asked leave to purchase two, one for the Duke of Cleveland, the other for Mr Plews, a director of the North of England Railway. The application was granted, but strict orders were given that no other papers should be sold."

So in Darlington, *The Northern Echo* had everything from the support of the town's leading businessmen to an in-built distribution advantage over all its competitors. And everyone in Darlington had something to gain from *The Northern Echo*: Bell developed his career, the Peases ensured their political message gained a wider audience. But, as *The Northern Echo's* first edition climbed aboard the early morning trains on New Year's Day, 1870, the Peases also got something that seems to have been just as important to them. They got one over their sworn local rival who in the previous five years had irritatingly dared to do to them what no other had for 50 years: challenge their superiority. So welcome *The Northern Echo*, the nation's first halfpenny morning, the country's first national daily, and perhaps the world's first newspaper born out of a game of one-upmanship.

3 A bright Spark

AT the time, Saturday, January 1, 1870, probably didn't seem like a red letter day to the people of Darlington. Despite all the hyperbole about the coming of the country's first halfpenny morning, it was, afterall, just another newspaper launch. For Darlington wasn't new to newspapers.

Indeed, when the Darlington Telegraph, General Advertiser and Servants Register had first been published in April 1854, its editorial began: "What! Another newspaper in Darlington?"

Although the Telegraph went on to reassure its readers that it was different from the rest – "No, not strictly a newspaper but a friend and a home companion, a periodical to warm the intellect of the labouring man, when his day of toil is finished" – Darlington's newspaper history already stretched back a century when the Echo was launched. The first publication had been J Sadler's tax-avoiding, remedy-peddling Darlington Pamphlet of 1772, which Sadler had followed up the following year with the Darlington Mercury. The Mercury, though, went the same way as the Pamphlet as it lasted only a few months after its debut on January 1, 1773.

In the heady post-tax days of 1855, a rash of publishing had broken out. The first was the Northern Express of April 21, but by the October it had fled to Newcastle where it was renamed the Northern Daily Express. By then, the Tees Mercury had risen and fallen – its one and only issue appeared in July 1855.

Next up was the Darlington Telegram which was published by Rapp and Dresser on High Row for a few months in 1858. In the same year, the Darlington Telegraph first appeared. It was remarkably long-lived, lasting under a different name until 1880.

Similarly, the North-East as a whole was littered with such short-lived projects: the Bishop Auckland Herald (1857-65), the Gateshead Observer (1837-86), the Shotley Bridge Times (1870-71) and the South Durham Herald (1866-91), to name but a few.

Of all these projects, the most enduring – and perhaps endearing – was the Darlington and Stockton Times which was first published on October 2, 1847, in Barnard Castle. And it was the dear old D&S, the sweet and venerated bible of the dalesman, that coughed up such bile and threw down such a challenge that the Pease family of Darlington were provoked into responding by creating *The Northern Echo*.

The D&S should, by rights, have been on the same side as the Peases and the Echo. It came from the same philanthropic roots. Its founder was George Brown, a highly-principled Barnard Castle barrister who wished to puncture the Tory monopoly of the press in the region, as achieved through the Durham Chronicle and Yorkshire Gazette. In his first editorial, Brown argued that the improvement of the conditions of the working class should be a non-party political issue, and in his prospectus prior to publication he had declared of the D&S: "In politics, it will labour to promote the diffusion of liberal principles, and the progress of peaceful and enlightened measures for the removal of national abuses, and for securing the just rights and privileges of all men, and the safety and welfare of the country."

When John Hyslop Bell came to write the prospectus for *The Northern Echo* 22 years later, he would echo many of Brown's promises for the D&S. But look again at that opening sentence of the opening paragraph of Bell's prospectus. Look again at his choice of words. *The Northern Echo* will be, says he, "a well-conducted, high-class Daily Newspaper, advocating Advanced Liberal opinions". But what, other than the addition of the word "daily", was there to differentiate this new-fangled Northern Echo from the well-established Darlington and Stockton Times which had been printing in Darlington since 1848? What need there a daily in Darnton when the D&S had effectively become bi-weekly in 1864 with the publication of its Wednesday morning sister paper, the Darlington Mercury? What need there another "well-conducted, high-class paper" in the sleepy town advocating more blesséd "advanced Liberal opinions" when the dear old D&S was all these things and more?

George Brown, founder of the D&S

Or perhaps, just perhaps, the D&S wasn't well-conducted. Perhaps it wasn't high-class. Perhaps its Liberal opinions were not quite as advanced as those of the Peases…

George Brown had lasted at the helm of the D&S only until February 1848 when the paper transferred to the basement of the Central Hall in Darlington. It now came under the control of Robert and William Thompson. They were reputable brothers based in Bondgate, sharebrokers, accountants and property developers. Thompson Street, which they built, still bears their name in the north end of Darlington.

But with the D&S to Darlington came an apprentice printer named Henry King Spark. And he became a big problem for the paper-less Peases.

Henry King Spark was the son of a miner from Alston in Cumbria. His mother, a schoolteacher, urged him to become a clergyman but when the family moved to Leeds he became an apprentice compositor in the printing trade. In 1847, now aged 22, he wound up in Barnard Castle, setting the type, reading the proofs and operating the press for Brown's Darlington and Stockton Times.

Spark wasn't best pleased with the paper's move to Darlington. He worked in the dingy basement of Central Hall and lived in dubious lodgings in Victoria Street, near the station. An advert on a proof caught his eye, and he landed a job as clerk to Mr Porter, coal and coke merchant on High Row.

Mysteriously, Porter soon fled Darlington, leaving Spark in sole command of a thriving business. He worked hard, touring the district, buying and selling coal. By either good luck or shrewd judgement, he found himself with a huge quantity of coal bought at the lowest price and suddenly in big demand as the economic climate changed.

On this one deal alone, he made a fortune – a reputed £30,000. He bought the Greenbank estate on the edge of Darlington, which was as magnificent a rural mansion as any owned by the Peases. It became the cultural and social centre of Darlington and he was widely known as the "Lord of Greenbank". In the late 1850s, he even began buying up collieries at Shincliffe and Houghall.

By 1862, though, Spark was experiencing financial difficulties and he turned to fellow mine-owner Joseph Love for assistance. The two went into partnership which alleviated Spark's worries and gave him surplus enough to buy the D&S when the Thompsons fell on hard times in 1864.

Still there shouldn't have been a problem. Spark was, afterall, a Liberal. But he was a maverick, and he set himself against Darlington's ruling Liberal clique, which revolved around the Pease family. The Peases were the creators of the railways and of Middlesbrough and Saltburn. They had fingers in every North-East pie from railway construction in Newcastle to iron ore extraction in North Yorkshire. Through wisely marrying within the Quaker faith, they had a network of family connections across the country that rivalled their network of railway connections across the region. It was the Peases and their acolytes – people like the Backhouse family who ran the bank on High Row – who ruled Darlington.

Yet Spark had the temerity to challenge them. And, in 1864, Spark had the one thing that the Peases did not have: a newspaper. He set about using the Darlington and Stockton Times as his platform to challenge the Peases. He then revived the Darlington Mercury as a mid-week reminder of his audacity.

Moving his papers to what he grandly called Printing House Square in Bondgate, he began campaigning for Darlington to become a Parliamentary borough and so return its own MP. This in itself didn't perturb the Peases too

*Henry King Spark,
owner of the D&S
and the fly in the
Peases' ointment*

much even though their people had represented the wider South Durham
constituency in Parliament since its creation in the Great Reform Act of 1832
when their most famous son, Joseph, had become Britain's first nonconformist
MP for 200 years. Indeed, given their local dominance, another seat at
Westminster meant another job for one of their cronies.

More worryingly for the Peases, though, was Spark's other campaign. In
1867, in the drawing-room of Greenbank, he drew up a petition that demanded
constitutional change within Darlington. Ten businessmen gave £10 each to
start the Charter Fund which demanded Darlington become a borough and gain
a proper town council to replace the Board of Health. He tapped into significant
public sympathy because there was a feeling in the town that the Board was not
running municipal affairs as well as it might.

But the Board was controlled by the Peases. In fact, it was almost their private
property: in the 1862 election the family alone had had 648 votes in a total of
7,678 cast.

So worried did the Peases become by the out-pourings in Spark's D&S and
Mercury that they decided to fight fire with fire. They took over Darlington's
only other existing newspaper, the Telegraph. In the editor's chair was Mark
Fooks. Fooks died in July 1917 and although his obituary in *The Northern Echo*
was strangely mute about the tumultuous times he had lived through, the tribute
in the Darlington and Stockton Times reveals much (this may be because in

1917 the D&S was independent and Conservative whereas the Echo was Liberal and its chairman, Arnold Rowntree, had impeccable Pease and Quaker credentials).

The obituary recalled: "Mr Fooks was first of all engaged on the Darlington Telegraph when it came into the hands of Messrs Burney. It was afterwards taken by the heads of what was at that time known as 'the Pease Party', who needed to be represented in opposition to the organs of Mr HK Spark – the Darlington and Stockton Times and the Darlington Mercury.

"A very fierce controversy arose from 1867 onwards, the old local and political parties resenting the attempts of Mr Spark to upset the current order of things. The opposing newspapers were the main factors in dealing with these issues, which were frequently not confined to principles involved, but developed into personalities of a most virulent type.

"Libels flew thick and fast, but no action was taken to stop this wordy war. The Spark party alleged what was little short of peculation on the part of the leading men on the opposite side." (For those without a turn of the century dictionary, peculation means "to take for one's own use money or property entrusted to one's care: to embezzle: to steal". Their noble Peases, common crooks?)

Continued the D&S: "For a time no notice was taken, but at length detailed statements were made. Mr Fooks then obtained special information and official data from local sources, and put the enemy to rout."

Fooks might have saved the honour of the Peases by routing Spark in the press, but in practice Spark proved successful. He spoke passionately from the platform in the Mechanics Hall in favour of reform and received wild acclaim while Joseph and John Pease, who had spoken against the reform, looked on gravely.

Both Spark's campaigns bore fruit. In 1867, Darlington was awarded its charter which meant that it had to elect its first town council. The first council meeting descended into a squabble. The Sparkites demanded that their hero, who had done so much to win the charter, should become mayor. But the Peases were having none of it, and amid great animosity chose Joseph Pease as Darlington's first mayor. Joseph was old and infirm so his brother, Henry, took the honour.

Yet Spark wasn't finished. In 1868, Darlington became a Parliamentary constituency, as Spark had called for, and now there was the matter of who would become the town's first MP.

Spark stood for election as an "independent Liberal". "The bitter feeling was renewed, and if possible intensified, when Darlington became a Parliamentary Borough, and Mr Spark became the opposing candidate to the old Liberal

Party's nominee," continued Fooks' obituary. That nominee was Edmund Backhouse, the head of the Quaker banking family inseparable from the Peases in most of their major business enterprises.

All mid-Victorian elections were disgracefully conducted, and the campaign of 1868 was no different. In the publicity stakes, Spark was way ahead, his bi-weekly double-header of the D&S and the Mercury giving him twice as much support as the Peases' once-a-week Telegraph. The D&S was even moved to rhyme:

"Mr Spark's been good for me,
I hope 'ere long he'll be our MP."

On a cold Monday morning in November, an ill-mannered crowd of 6,000 gathered before the hustings from which Spark and Backhouse spoke. The eloquent Spark won hands down, and when a show of hands was called, they were mostly raised in his favour. He was on the verge of being declared elected when Backhouse called for a written poll, to which he was legally entitled. This was held on the Friday, and Backhouse triumphed by 1,789 votes to 872.

In Saturday's D&S, Spark fumed: "On Monday morning a show of hands more magnificent as regards numbers than any show of hands that has yet been displayed in Darlington was held up in favour of Mr Spark. Mr Spark represented freedom. Mr Spark represented independence. Unfortunately freedom and independence were a dead letter in Darlington yesterday. From street to street, from ward to ward, the screw was imposed with the most unblushing audacity. Early in the morning, ward after ward was visited, and in ward after ward, the screw was unmistakably present."

Edmund Backhouse, representative
of the Pease Party

This close shave with humiliation in their own backyard taught the mighty Peases a lesson or two: never underestimate the power of the press and, when all else fails, make sure you own your own newspaper. Best of all, make sure your paper appears every morning to drown out the noise of your weekly competitors and make sure that it covers as wide an area as possible so that should you encounter a maverick whose interests stretch throughout the county, he can be shouted down with authority.

Within ten months of the 1868 General Election, John Hyslop Bell had been invited to Darlington; within 14 months of the Election, *The Northern Echo* was on the streets of Darlington, a "well-conducted, high-class paper" "advocating "Advanced Liberal opinions" in the manner of the Peases themselves. Surely not a coincidence. And neither was it a coincidence that the first sub-editor of *The Northern Echo* should be Mark Fooks, the man who'd done so much on the Telegraph to save the Peases' blushes.

But the story of the Echo versus the D&S, of the Peases versus Henry King Spark doesn't end there. And as the remaining chapters unfold, the true nature of the Spark, the devil that the Peases founded *The Northern Echo* to attack, becomes clear.

After the 1868 Election, Spark was still the idol of the working-classes of Darlington, partly because he had dared to challenge the ruling interests and partly because of his ventures like the Drinkfield Ironworks which he was attempting to run on a visionary co-operative basis. In 1869, 3,000 workers paid for Spark to be presented with a lifesize oil-painting of himself which he, in a kindly gesture, presented to the town council. Both the gesture and the painting, though, were acts of self-aggrandisement: it later transpired that Spark himself had secretly given most of the money to the painting fund.

His business partner, Joseph Love, was all too aware of Spark's eccentricities. He was also concerned by his erratic business ventures – like the Merrybent railway which opened in 1870, never made a profit and later became the route of the A1(M) which bypassed Darlington in the 1960s – and personal gambling habits. Love bought Spark out of the partnership and, in 1872, with money worries crowding in on him, Spark launched a scurrilous writ against Love. In the same year, he merged his Wednesday Mercury paper with his Saturday Darlington and Stockton Times.

Even with the morning might of *The Northern Echo* ranged against him and his weekly mouthpiece, Spark again stood against Backhouse in the 1874 Election. It was another contest coloured by calumny and it proved to be closer than the 1868 result. It was confused by the last-minute arrival of a Conservative candidate, Thomas Gibson Bowles, a London solicitor who edited the Vanity Fayre magazine. The result gave Backhouse a wafer-thin victory:

Backhouse (Lib) 1,625
Spark (Inde Lib) 1,607
Bowles (Con)   302

Again Spark railed against the result in the D&S, and with some justification for he had stood against a party machine powered by all the resources the Peases could throw at it. Again Spark accused them of underhand methods, of peculation, of turning the screw on reluctant voters.

A contemporary cartoon from the 1868 election. Taken from Shakespeare's Julius Caesar, "slightly altered from the original text", Brutus (left) is played by HK S***k and Cassius (right) by E B*ckh**se. While Brutus holds a copy of the Darlington & Stockton Times, he says: "That you have wrong'd me doth appear in this."

"Here was a great party with all the power that wealth, influence and position could give them," he fumed in the D&S. "They had all the appliances known to electioneering craft... They bought up all the lawyers they could get hold of... They had gangs of canvassers scouring every street and alley in the borough...

"Yet with all these means and appliances on one side, and the absence of them on the other, the nominee of the great Quaker party was only fluked in at the last moment by a majority of 18 votes."

Spark had a point, for one of the greatest appliances ranged against him was *The Northern Echo*. And this was the 1874 Election in which, under its vivacious new editor WT Stead, *The Northern Echo* achieved its first success as a campaigning newspaper. It had fearlessly championed the Liberal cause when the rest of the country was deserting it. Elsewhere, the Liberals were humiliated at the polls and unceremoniously ejected from power. But in County Durham, where *The Northern Echo* was strongest, all 13 of the MPs returned were Liberals. So proud of its achievement was the Echo that it printed elaborate profiles of the "Durham 13" in the paper. Then it rushed them out in a handsome volume as a tribute to the 'triumph'.

The introduction to the 155-page book was probably written by Stead himself as it is signed "Northern Echo Office, Darlington, 8th April 1874." It reads: "The General Election of 1868 gave the Liberal party a majority of 110. That of 1874 left them in a minority of 49. This unprecedented transfer of political power was the result of a disaffection existing in almost every part of the United Kingdom, excepting the county of Durham. When 'Conservative Reaction' was acknowledged supreme over the rest of the country, the County Palatine returned to the House of Commons, for the first time since 1832, an unbroken band of Liberal members. As a memorial to this remarkable triumph, these sketches of the Durham Thirteen – which first appeared in the only morning daily newspaper in the county – are now collected in a form somewhat less ephemeral than that in which they were first laid before the public."

One of the Durham 13 was, of course, Edmund Backhouse who had scraped home by 18 against the maverick independent Spark. The chapter dedicated to Backhouse in *The Northern Echo's* book goes to great lengths to explain how this apparent narrow squeak was in fact a great victory. It blames the appearance of the Conservative for costing Backhouse 300 votes; it blames the Catholics, who had been tempted by Spark's "artful tactics", for costing Backhouse 700 votes; and it blames the 350 newly-enfranchised voters for being naive enough to be lured by Spark's lurid rhetoric.

"That Mr Spark should gain by the new electors was natural enough," reasoned the Echo. "He had been carefully nursing the constituency since the first election. Mr Backhouse, unfortunately resided out of town (in Middleton Tyas), and he could not throw open his grounds to the holiday-makers. Mr Spark did, and gained much popularity thereby. Mr Backhouse's peculiar claims to support, his intellectual ability, his financial skill, and his invaluable services, were neither known nor appreciated by strangers, who judged of the men only by their professions on the platform. The marvel is that the sitting member should have gained so largely from the electors lately added to the register, not that he should have been distanced among the strangers by a candidate who had never ceased electioneering since last election."

It is hard not to feel that somehow, just a little, the Echo doth protest too much about the overwhelming triumph that lay behind Backhouse's slim majority. It seems to be saying that if Backhouse's peculiar claims as put forward by *The Northern Echo* had not been drowned out by the rattling of the D&S, he would have won handsomely. In fact, he would have routed Spark by 2,600 votes to 900 if that bounder hadn't campaigned before and during the election ("in electioneering, Mr Backhouse believes that the innocence of the dove is better than the wisdom of the serpent"). Indeed, he would have won by 3,500 to zero if the Tories and the Catholics had voted for him – as they jolly well should have done. But Stead (for surely 'tis he) has an answer for that Shakespearian allegation, too. He finishes his sketch: "We have been a little careful to explain this matter, since persons who are ignorant of local politics might naturally enough imagine that a majority under open voting of 927, reduced under the Ballot to 18, savoured undue influence. No one who knows Mr Backhouse could for a moment suspect him capable of using the smallest pressure to secure the votes of political opponents. His one failing as a candidate is the fact that he will not even use the friendly pressure that would stimulate the energies of his numerous friends."

So, absolutely no peculation there, then.

Even without this incisive dissection of his overwhelming defeat, Spark had problems – largely of the financial kind. After the election he was forced to sell Greenbank and his far-fetched pursuit of Joseph Love through the courts became so grievous that Love, an old man, died. In 1876, Spark was forced to file a petition for bankruptcy in the Cumberland County Court. He claimed to have assets of £335,997 but the liquidator valued them at just £2,350 – all but £350 of which was made up by Spark's "newspaper property".

Now, at his weakest moment, the Echo and its backers were able to gain the ultimate revenge. In 1878, the trustees of Spark's estate forced him to sell his beloved Darlington and Stockton Times, the paper on which, back in 1847 in Barnard Castle, he had started his career.

The new purchasers of the paper were, naturally, a group of Liberals. Leading the group was none other than John Hyslop Bell (founder and sole proprietor of the Echo). Other members included Sir David Dale (soon to become chairman of the Echo), Sir Joseph Whitwell Pease (official Liberal MP for South Durham, one of the Durham 13 and effectively the head of the Pease family) and Henry Fell Pease (son of the man Spark had bitterly opposed as first Darlington mayor).

To lesser mortals, this would have been the final indignity. But not to Henry King Spark. Now with no newspaper backing, he stood in the 1880 General Election and once again took on the Peases' preferred candidate, Theodore Fry.

The election came when his fortunes were at an all-time low. Joseph Love's widow had taken up the cudgels and demanded that Spark justify all the allegations in court that he made against her late husband – especially the one that Love had robbed him of a million pounds.

The Vice-Chancellor hearing the case was not impressed. He told Spark: "The poor old man (Love) was 75; you saw him go to 80 before you filed your bill. The poor old man is harassed out of his life. He puts in his answer and expires. I am not inclined to give Mr Spark one hour more. He delays five years and then files the most offensive bill without exception I have ever read, and now you are worrying the widow. It looks very bad."

To fight the 1880 Election, the Peases again turned to their newspaper armoury which by now was well-equipped: the Echo, the D&S, and the Darlington Telegraph. The Telegraph had been kept well behind the lines since the Peases had belatedly turned to it in 1867 to see off the Spark threat first time around. Now they dusted it down and oiled it ready for action to see off the Spark threat in what proved to be the last battle of a 15-year war.

The Telegraph had been renamed the Darlington and Richmond Herald in 1873 and its sole proprietor chose the very eve of the 1880 poll to enumerate every single one of Spark's business and personal failings.

The sole proprietor of the Herald was, of course, John Hyslop Bell, the founder of *The Northern Echo*. Bell ended his cannon blast against Spark with the conclusion that independent candidate was "an undischarged bankrupt and vainglorious braggard".

It was a fatal shot. Fry won by 2,772 votes to Spark's 1,331.

Spark was extinguished. Heavily in debt, his newspaper and political careers in shreds, he slunk away to Startforth near Barnard Castle. He became involved in local churches and rehabilitated his reputation enough to be elected to the Teesdale Board of Guardians and become a good friend to the poor and under-privileged of the market town.

On the afternoon of November 22, 1899, he attended a Board of Guardians meeting and then returned to his home, The Mount, which as he was a bachelor he shared only with housekeeper. That evening, he bade her goodnight. "I am tired," he said, and collapsed and expired before he could reach his bedroom. He was 75.

Spark was not the only casualty of the 1880 Election. In destroying his chances, the Darlington and Richmond Herald (neé Darlington Telegraph) had fired its last shot. Shortly after the Election, it was retired from active service, never to appear again. This left Darlington served by two papers: *The Northern Echo* and the weekly Darlington and Stockton Times. Both were owned by the town's Liberal establishment – but its former owner's independent streak had rubbed off on the impudent little weekly and it still had a couple of nasty nips to deliver to its bigger sister before it could be properly welcomed into the Priestgate stable.

4 No 1

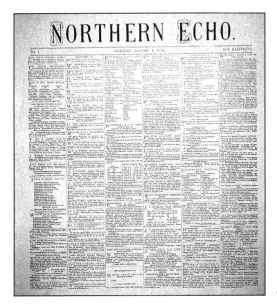

*The first page of
the first edition of
January 1, 1870*

ACTS are a newspaper's lifeblood. They are it's stock-in-trade. "Always check your facts," every trainee journalist has drummed into them. "Never assume anything."

So having established the first big fact about *The Northern Echo* – that it was founded on January 1, 1870, by John Hyslop Bell – it is a little embarrassing to come to the second big fact: the name of the first editor.

He was probably Mr Coplestone. Or he could have been Copplestone. Or Coppelstone. Or Copelstone. Or Coblestone. Or Cobblestone. But it is safest to assume that he was Coplestone – if only because WT Stead refers to him as such in the paper on September 23, 1871 (however, five months earlier Stead had referred to him in a letter as Mr Copleston but that was before he had met him and before he had become a journalist who always checks his facts).

We know for an incontrovertible fact, though, that the Christian name of the first editor was John.

John Coplestone seems to have come to Darlington from the Morning Star in London. His sub-editor – possibly his deputy editor and probably his only other journalist – was Mark Fooks. Fooks had been born near Sherbourne in Dorset and had worked on papers in Banbury, Oxford, Macclesfield, Chesterfield and

Brighton before coming to Richmond in 1859 to edit the Richmond and Ripon Chronicle. In 1865 he had moved to Darlington to start a connection with the town's newspapers that was to last 46 years. His first post was probably as editor of the Darlington Telegraph which, in the middle of the first Spark crisis, had been taken over by the Pease Party. Fooks' reward for routing Spark was a job on *The Northern Echo*.

Together, Coplestone and Fooks, with Bell hovering somewhere in the background, produced the first edition of *The Northern Echo* on "the Natal Day of the New Year", as they called it in their first leader. That leader started with Old Moore's prediction that "1870 will be one of the happiest years the world has known" and concluded by saying that 1870 would turn out to be one of the busiest years Parliament had ever known. Inbetween, the leader discussed the affairs of Europe, the Irish Church Bill and the prospect of the Forster Education Act. It also launched into a campaign to get the postal rate for newspapers and printed matter reduced from 1d to ½d – a campaign close to this halfpenny's heart because it also praised the North-Eastern Railway Company for choosing the Natal Day to drop its prices. In the same way that the Echo would gain sales by costing just a halfpenny, the Royal Mail would find itself handling more letters if it dropped its rates and so the railways would find more people using its services, argued the leader. Also, of course, the Echo would be able to distribute itself more cheaply by both mail and rail.

John Boyd, the Echo's first printer, and his wife Winifred

The first issue of *The Northern Echo* consisted of four pages 34cms by 40cms printed on a flatbed "four-feeder" press in Priestgate at the rate of 1,500 pages an hour. The first printer was John Boyd who came with Bell from the South Durham and Cleveland Mercury. Despite his age – Boyd cannot yet have been 20 – Bell had entrusted him to go to Otley to examine the press before it was installed in Priestgate.

This suggests Boyd printed the first edition of *The Northern Echo* – the very first copy of which he kept under the cushion on his fireside cane chair in his apartment at the ED Walker Homes where he died aged 83 in the mid-1930s – on a secondhand press.

Page one of that first edition consisted entirely of small adverts placed by businessmen from Darlington (Oliver the printer in Tubwell Row), Sunderland (William Wade's India Rubber Depot in High Street West), Newcastle (Dickinson the tobacconist in the Bigg Market), Saltburn (W Taylor, surgeon-dentist) and West Hartlepool (GW Young, hat manufacturer in New Market), to name just a few.

Page two opened with property adverts – 16 houses for sale in Albert Hill, £150 deposit required – and notices from the Hartlepool Port and Harbour Commissioners. There was a heartfelt plea from Mrs Binney of Eastbourne, Darlington, who "will be obliged to the lady who borrowed a book entitled Money to return the same as soon as possible". There was also a plea from Edward Pease, wintering in Torquay, in the paper's first letter. He asked ratepayers to support his idea for a public library, but as there were eight private libraries attached to churches in the town – plus Mrs Binney's collection even if it was without Money – there wasn't much enthusiasm among ratepayers for another burden upon them (it wasn't until Edward died in 1880 leaving a bequest that his project became a possibility. The Edward Pease Memorial Library opened opposite the Echo's Priestgate office in 1884).

Page two also includes a list of local share prices, provided by the Darlington and Stockton Times' former owner, Robert Thompson, and an article on the Cleveland pig iron trade. The Echo's prospectus states that such "impartial, authoritative and sound Commercial News" would be supplied by "a City Editor of established reputation" which was presumably Fooks who was a specialist in this field.

After the commercial news, the leader begins, spilling over onto page three on which some local shorts are printed: Assault by a commercial traveller at Middlesbrough; The Foot and Mouth Disease and the defence of Hartlepool; Alleged theft of a watch at Langbaurgh and a weather update. "The thaw has been very rapid, insomuch that most of the snow in the neighbourhood of Darlington has now disappeared. The rivers have in consequence become very much swollen, and in some places have passed their banks. This is the case with both the Tees and the Skerne."

These shorts were probably the work of the Echo's first team of reporters. The prospectus said that "professional reporters will daily calendar meetings and occurrences of local interest in Middlesbrough, Stockton, the Hartlepools, Darlington, the Aucklands and Barnard Castle", but it is difficult to judge how many editorial staff the early Echo really had. Fooks recalled that "there were critical occasions when Stead was known to have written half the paper himself", but on September 23, 1871, the Echo reported that Michael Graham, its "chief reporter at Darlington", was leaving to study theology at Durham University. A

Laying the library's foundation stone in 1884 in Crown Street with the Echo's office clearly behind

chief reporter, one would assume, must have had some less-than-chief reporters to order around.

Presumably, then, it was these subordinates who had wandered down to the Tees and the Skerne to check on the water levels. Following their reports on page three, there were up-dates from France, Spain, Portugal, America, Ireland, the Danubian Principalities and news from Russia: "The disease from which the Emperor is suffering, the Lancet says, is hypochondriasis – a malady which is hereditary in the Imperial family of Russia." This may be a joke.

Page three also included the paper's sports coverage – two paragraphs about horse racing at Thirsk – and the day's fixtures – where and when the hunt would meet.

Page four opened with a lengthy report on the Ladies' Association for Repealing the Contagious Diseases Act. It carried a few local engagements – Mr Backhouse MP will preside at an open conference of working men at the Mechanics Institute in Darlington next Tuesday – and a births, marriages and deaths section (even then, the deaths out-weighed the births by three to one), and a wanted column for people seeking accommodation or employment. Page four concluded with shipping intelligence from around the world.

This page, though, reveals much about *The Northern Echo*, including its advertising rates.

"If you want –
A SITUATION as cook or housemaid, or laundry-maid or seniliery-maid; an butler, or coachman, or groom; as manager, or accountant, or clerk, warehouseman, or light or heavy porter:
LODGINGS, or to let lodgings,
A HOUSE or to let one;
A SERVANT of any kind, a domestic, a clerk, an accountant, a cashier: – ADVERTISE IN *The Northern Echo*. TWENTY WORDS FOR SIXPENCE."

The paper also carried a notice for newsagents: "Unlimited supplies of *The Northern Echo* may be had at the usual half price for publication by application. Those applications had to be made to its special agents who were at Stockton, Hartlepool, Middlesbrough, West Hartlepool, Whitby, Sunderland, Newcastle, York, Bishop Auckland and Barnard Castle." Plus, of course, the Darlington special agent who organised all distribution from the Old Post Office in Northgate.

There followed a list of 62 ordinary agents, mainly station masters and newsagents, who also sold *The Northern Echo* from Bedale to Yarm. As well as newsagents selling the first edition, in Darlington the Town Bellman wandered around the streets advertising the new paper and recruiting young boys to sell it.

There is one other revealing notice tucked away in the 'wanted' section of page four of No 1: "Wanted: an eight or ten-bedroomed house in the Cockerton Road direction. Apply to JC, Echo Offices."

Was that JC the editor, John Coplestone, in search of accommodation? It is to be hoped that if it was him, he took his house on a short term lease because even in those days it was a precarious business being an editor.

Within 16 months of No 1 appearing, the Echo had established its name. Fortuitously, it was founded during a war, the Franco-Prussian War, and through its network of "special sources" whose reports were wired to Darlington by telegraphy, the Echo provided an accurate and immediate account of how Prussia defeated France. As WT Stead wrote in 1874: "*The Northern Echo* first gained distinction by its early intelligence, partly from special sources of information, during the Franco-German War of 1870-71."

But, despite this success, at the end of those 16 months Coplestone was sacked. Little is known of his departure other than in early April 1871 he had had a major disagreement with Bell and that he later emigrated to America. Even before the April, though, Bell had been manoeuvring behind Coplestone's back to find a replacement. The man who was to take Coplestone's place in the editor's chair was to make the Echo famous, both nationally and internationally.

5 Turning a young man's head

WT Stead, editor 1871-1880

AN article comparing the administrative institutions of America with those of Britain and discussing the place of Christianity in a democracy may not sound like required reading. But to *The Northern Echo's* founder John Hyslop Bell it was.

It appeared while Bell was abroad and he determined to find out more about its writer when he returned to Darlington.

On entering the former thread factory in Priestgate, Bell was told – presumably by his editor John Coplestone – that the author was a young chap from Newcastle called William Thomas Stead. Indeed, so impressed was Bell by the article that on Saturday April 8, 1871, unbeknown to Coplestone, he ventured north to Newcastle to ask Stead to become the new editor of *The Northern Echo*.

Bell met the 21-year-old protege in his office at 27 Broad Chare on the Quayside.

Stead, who had been born on July 5, 1849, at Embleton near Alnwick, had been employed as a clerk in Charles Septimus Smith's shipping office on the Quayside since he the age of 14. Smith was also the Russian vice-consul, acting on behalf of Russian ships calling at the Quayside, and this certainly shaped the young Stead. Britain was gripped by a fear of Russia, a vast, unknown and secretive empire in the east that had designs on Britain's dominance and trade connections, but Stead's early involvement with Russian sailors indicated to him that there was little to fear.

When Smith became Mayor of Newcastle, he discovered his young employee shared many of his concerns about local social conditions and Stead began writing his speeches.

Stead was also writing for newspapers. In 1865, his first leading article was published in what his daughter Estelle remembered as "a little Jarrow weekly paper" (either the Jarrow Guardian or the Jarrow Express). It was about the assassination of President Lincoln. His second leader came in 1868. It was for the Sheffield Independent on the subject of the disestablishment of the Irish Church.

He was also writing to newspapers. His first letter was sent to the Northern Daily Express in Newcastle. It was inspired by an unfortunate encounter with a ruffian. Throughout his life, Stead was known as a soft touch by those wanting money and on his daily walk to work on the Quayside, he had become acquainted with a beggar. Eventually, Stead decided to give the fellow his best overcoat – on condition that the beggar read every night the bible he was also giving him. The beggar immediately returned to his lodgings, stole everything he could lay his hands on and headed off into the night, wearing the overcoat but leaving the bible.

Stead was shocked and upset. He wrote to the Northern Daily Express demanding that a Mendacity Society be formed to help the real people in need and to weed out the cheats. When the letter was published, he sent marked copies of it to leading members of Newcastle's civic society. He aroused enough interest to hold a town meeting out of which a Mendacity Society was formed.

As well as writing to and for newspapers, Stead was writing to his girlfriend. He was still living with his parents in Embleton near Alnwick. Unsurprisingly for someone who had been educated on the knee of his father, a Congregational minister, so that by the age of six he could recite Latin grammar, the teenage Stead struggled with girls. Then the Embleton doctor's sister came to stay for the summer. She was at least ten years older than Stead but, as he admitted, the lack of diversions in the village led her to take an interest in the studious youth. Stead was infatuated. She was "the only woman I have ever turned over music for at the piano...the first woman to whom I ever said the word love".

When the summer faded, the doctor's sister returned to Edinburgh and Stead wrote her "immense letters three times a week". He drove himself to make each one better than the last to meet her exacting standards. In 1868, after his article in the Sheffield Independent, the strain of his letter-writing caused him to suffer nervous exhaustion which gave him such eye problems that he wasn't able to write for 18 months.

And so his girl was lost, but he had learned to write. "I often advise young people who come to me now and ask what would be the best school in which to learn to write well," he said later. "(It is) to fall in love with a clever woman a dozen years older than yourselves who lives a distance from you and with whom you can only communicate by writing."

He recovered both his heart and his sight early in 1870 and began trying the newly-formed Liberal paper in Darlington. He sent a letter about organisation to Coplestone who wrote back thanking him and saying he would publish it. "But he did not put it in exactly as it was written," complained Stead. "He put in several sentences of his own from which I dissented and I wrote to tell him so. This brought about a correspondence and he asked me to write more."

Stead's first assignment was probably the Social Science Congress in Newcastle in September 1870. Whereas the Newcastle Chronicle was able to send a substantial team of reporters to the Congress, Stead was the Echo's sole representative. Yet he was able to stamp a distinctive style on his reports which were far more colourful and atmospheric than the conventional way of covering such sober events. Stead reported: "The teetotallers then had a field day, and kept thundering away at intoxicating liquors, until the great bulk of the members of the association left town to drink wine with Mr Palmer, after the inspection of Messrs Allhusen's Chemical Works." (Stead's ambivalence towards the teetotallers may be explained by the fact that he enjoyed the very rare half-a-pint of stout and smoked the occasional cigar; he also took six lumps of sugar in his tea.)

More assignments followed. Stead recalled: "After having written for about nine months I modestly ventured to suggest that as I was writing about three leaders a week, and half-a-dozen occasional notes, the labourer might be worthy of his hire! The editor replied saying he was sorry, but there was no fund available to pay outside contributors, and that if I insisted upon payment he would just have to fall back on his own unaided pen.

"He sent me a book by Miss Yonge, with a shorthand inscription which I could not understand (having no knowledge of shorthand), but which I afterwards learnt was the prayer: 'May your Soul be bound up in the Bundle of Life.' And that was the only payment – if payment it may be called."

Stead might have been doing Coplestone a disservice for at one point it appears that the editor told his contributor that if he wished to write something for a London paper which paid for articles, he would sub-edit it and make sure it got printed.

The wrankles over payment disappeared when Bell came calling on April 8. After a couple of hours the proprietor offered Stead the editor's chair. The salary was to be £150 in the first year "when I would need an experienced sub, £250 in the second when I could do without such a high class sub and content myself with a cheaper article". He was also to be guaranteed a fortnight's holiday a year.

Stead asked for time to consider. He said he would have to write to Coplestone (or Copleston as he was still calling him) "as he was my friend". This seems to have shaken Bell because he had yet to tell his founding editor that he was about to be sacked.

Stead also consulted with his father, who advised him not to go, and wrote to the only other person he knew in Darlington, the Reverend Henry Kendall, asking him for advice, too. Kendall was the pastor of the Congregational Church in Union Street (today a carpet shop). Originally from Lincolnshire, Kendall had delivered his first sermon at the tender age of 11 years and eight months and had become something of a religious freak show touring under the name of "the Boy Preacher". After a short time in Sunderland, he had settled in Darlington in 1859 where he died at his home in Stanhope Road aged 68 in 1900. His obituary says that he was "the doyen of Nonconformist ministers in Darlington and district" and it is probable that Stead knew him through his father, also a Congregationalist minister, and through Kendall's numerous articles in magazines like Methodist Quarterly.

Stead was quite specific in the advice he sought from the Rev Kendall (although, mirroring his difficulties with Coplestone, he misspelled the pastor's name Kendal in his letter). Should he, a decent God-fearing man, be prepared to work from 7pm on Sunday nights preparing the Monday morning paper? Where would he be able to find lodgings with gas? And what was this Northern Echo paper like? "What (do) you think is the probability of the Echo existing and

WT Stead's letter to the Rev Henry Kendall

Stead's chair is still in the office of the Editor of **The Northern Echo**, *although there is some doubt about its authenticity. From here he began attacking the devil*

getting on? It would be miserable to be tied up with a bankruptcy affair."

Although the letter to Kendall is framed and occupying pride of place in office of today's editor of *The Northern Echo*, we do not know of the contents of the reply. Perhaps the good vicar said that Sunday working was out of the question because Stead's contract released him from such duties and said he did not have to work after nine o'clock at night – however, Stead the stickler would often be found at his desk on a Sunday after nine.

However, the tone of Stead's letter suggests that no matter what the reverend gentleman said, the young man's mind was made up.

"Just think, your humble servant editor of the Echo with an experienced man of 40 below him as a sub and WT Stead being only 22. It is enough to turn a fellow's head," he wrote.

"I never dreamed of such an elevation so easily. I should have also…control over what I wrote and about what I wrote only providing I am Liberal, non conformist, free trade. All of which I am of course. What a glorious opportunity of attacking the devil isn't it?"

He took the job. Coplestone left that April and later emigrated to America. By August, Stead was installed in his famous chair and, with Fooks as his experienced sub-editor, set about attacking the devil with gusto.

6 Attacking the devil

STEAD was soon into his stride, laying into any number of devils. "What a glare, lurid as the fiery rain that licked up the doomed cities of Sodom and Gomorrah, does that one awful fact cast over Christian England," he said in an editorial in November 1871 with fire and brimstone pouring from his pen.

His subject was prostitution – "the ghastliest curse which haunts civilised society, which is steadily sapping the very foundations of our morality". It was a subject that would later make his name notorious and put him in prison.

Even in 1871, just three months into his first newspaper job, he already had answers. "Until all classes set themselves in earnest to root out all customs whether promiscuous dancing or occasional drinking, which produce and foster the prevailing laxity of morals; and until the tone of society is so improved that a man who tampers with female purity is shunned as carefully as if he were a convicted assassin; we fear that the best efforts of philanthropists will be of no avail in stemming this bitterest scourge of our race."

He went further. Prostitution was not an isolated scourge. The whole of society, he claimed was, "outwardly appears white and glistening...but within is full of dead men's bones and rottenness".

The other topic by which he was to make his name was his love of Russia, and he also rehearsed his Russophile arguments in his early days. Britain was scared of Russia invading Persia, a country Britain saw as a vital buffer between Russia's expansionist ideas and her empire in India, whereas Russia saw Persia as a useful supplier of raw cotton with strategically placed seaports on the Gulf. Stead, unlike much of his readership, sided with Russia. In 1873, he wrote antagonistically for a British audience which liked to think its imperialist ways were bringing civilisation to savages: "With all her faults, Russia civilizes...it appears to us that when we forbid Russia to conquer Khiva or Persia, we are virtually acting the part of bitter foes to civilisation."

There were other topics. In 1871, after a Tyneside engineering strike he called for the trials of strength between owners and workers which usually solved industrial disputes to be replaced by a Board of Arbitration; in 1874, after three men were executed at Durham Jail for their part in a brutal killing, he spoke out against those who advocated the abolition of hanging.

These latter two topics saw Stead come into direct conflict with the views of the "Pease Party". Said Stead in 1893: "I preached just the same as I preach now, advocating Industrial Arbitration and Imperial Extension, much to the horror of the good Quakers who found, I believe, the money with which the Echo was established. I was also heretic on the subject of Capital Punishment."

Stead was also in conflict with Bell – he wouldn't wear a top hat to work despite the proprietor's requests!

But Bell and the Quakers kept faith with Stead. He was, afterall, staunchly Liberal. Tories were the children of hell and their leader, Benjamin Disraeli, was the devil himself. In March 1873, a year before William Gladstone's first Government ended in a cataclysmic Conservative landslide, Stead wrote this glowing paeon of praise to the Prime Minister's works: "It is not for us to write the epitaph of the expiring administration. That will be written in letters of gold by the future historians of England, and for many a year hereafter, we shall trace loving tributes to its beneficent sway, written in lustrous characters of sunlight upon every institution of our common country."

And, reasoned Bell and the Quakers, the impetuous youth who was the youngest editor in the country, was beginning to mature. When he came to Darlington Stead rented Flora Cottage off Victoria Road on the Polam Hall estate but, as he prepared for marriage to his childhood sweetheart (before the doctor's sister) Emma Lucy Wilson from Howdon, he took rooms in Darlington town centre. The terraced streets he could now see were decidedly working class, but he detested the "rows of slated hideousness" and covered his windows with blinds to shut out the view.

Marriage in 1874 saw him move to Grainey Hill Cottage on the Hummersknott estate. It was far more rural and to his liking – it had previously been called Viewly House because of its excellent aspect overlooking the Tees valley – and there he kept bees, rabbits, dogs, a goat and a pony.

The pony became a trademark, the noise from its hooves shattering the peace of the rows of terraced houses as he rode home in the early mornings after a hard day's editing. He tethered the pony, along with his dogs, to a stone – a cheese press – which is still in Crown Street.

The young father – his children born at Grainey Hill were Willie in 1874, Harry in 1875, Alfred in 1877 and Emma (known as Estelle) in 1879 – was clearly happy with his life. Later he reminisced: "Living two miles out of Darlington we saw few visitors. I rode into town after dark, returning at two or three in the morning. The life of the little household was well under way before I awoke, but all the rest of the day we spent together."

Every year on his birthday he wrote a letter to himself. As he turned 26 in 1875 he contentedly reflected: "As to the paper, I am better satisfied with it than ever. It has the first position in the district. We now reach 13,000 (people); we may reach 20,000. To address 20,000 people as the sole preacher is better than to be a tenth part of the preaching power on a journal with 200,000 circulation. There is no paper now in existence which can be to me what the Echo is. I have given it its character, its existence, its circulation. It is myself. Other papers could not bear my image and superscription so distinctly."

In fact, the paper was developing quite nicely. In March 1873, the pages became three-and-a-half inches longer and although most of the additional space was devoted to advertisements, the extra revenue paid for a London office to be opened in Fleet Street in 1874.

Stead's 1875 birthday letter concludes happily: "In money of course it is not much, but it is enough to keep me comfortable, and Bell has promised me a share in profit hereafter. I think I shall stop here. All signs are for it."

He was a big noise in his own district, but the events of 1876 were to catapult him – and the Echo – to national and international prominence. "Until the advent of the Eastern Question, Mr Stead had not achieved more than a local reputation in connection with *The Northern Echo*, recalled his loyal deputy,"

The stone to which Stead tethered his pony is now opposite the Priestgate Office

Mark Fooks. "The intensity of his political convictions, as shown by the fervour of his writings, had been previously manifest to Liberal political circles in Durham and Yorkshire and adjacent counties. The advent of the struggle between Russia and Turkey...first brought Mr Stead into recognition amongst the leading statesmen of the Liberal party."

The Eastern Question again saw Stead's favourite foreign nation, Russia, in conflict with British interests. Having been partially successful in Persia, the Tsar now turned his attention to the Balkans. He began promoting the concept of "pan-Slavism" which united all the Slav nations in an independent utopia headed by Russia. But most Slav territories were ruled by the crumbling Ottoman Empire (Turkey) with which Britain had important trade ties. Disraeli, the Prime Minister, preferred to do little other than support the Turks. From late 1875, Stead was prophesying that this would be a disastrous policy and in April 1876, he was proved right. There was a nationalist uprising in Bulgaria which was ruthlessly put down by the Sultan. As many as 12,000 Bulgarians were massacred horribly – babies were speared, men and women were impaled on poles and left writhing to die.

Stead was outraged. "Blazing villages, massacred multitudes, enslaved children, outraged maidens, he screamed. "The unbridled licence of Asiatic savagery...

"The Premier has betrayed the cause of humanity to purse the glittering bubble of ambition.

"We are branded before Europe as responsible for atrocities worthy of the Tartar despot who piled a pyramid of 90,000 gory skulls at the gates of Damascus...

"As the Bashi-Bazouk and the Turk and the Circassian went forth to massacre matrons, toss babies upon their bayonets and inflict the most bestial outrages upon Christian maidens their war cry was: 'Death to the Ghiaours, the English are on our side!'

"You might expect the election of a new Pope to convert the Roman Catholic Church to Wesleyan Methodism as to expect the accession of a new Sultan to do justice to the Christians in the East.

"It may be right to check Russia. It is not right to support as a means to that end a government (Disraeli's) which is not merely a negation of God but a palpable affirmation of the Devil."

Stead was not content in merely railing from his ivory tower. He set to work. He had faith in the people of the North-East – "the home of all good causes", he said – to rally to the cause, despite his critics. "Witlings, cynics and the whole tribes of moral eunuchs who are only too numerous in many quarters infest the North like other vermin," he wrote, "but they are recognised as vermin."

On August 25, he held his first "Atrocity Meeting" in Darlington. "We look to the men of Darlington to sing again the heroic note of Milton's sonnet; and we look to the men of the North to repeat the strains until it is thundered by a million voices in the ears of recreant Ministers," he wrote.

Within a week, Stead had cajoled all the important people he knew in the district to attend Atrocity Meetings and to organise their own gatherings in towns and villages. "The North is up," he wrote. "What was a storm in a teacup is now a tempest sweeping through the length and breadth of the land.

And he was right. Britain was aflame with moral outrage. Stead's fortnight of agitation had done more to stop the Turkish killings than three months of diplomacy by Disraeli.

Just as importantly, Stead had re-awoken Gladstone. Defeated in the 1874 Election – despite the triumph of the Durham 13 – Gladstone had practically retired from public affairs in January 1875, his Liberal party split, disillusioned and in need of a spark to reunite it and draw Gladstone back into the fray. Stead provided that spark. He sent Gladstone early copies of *The Northern Echo* which included his trenchant articles and he persuaded the Atrocity Meetings in the North-East to call for Gladstone to take up the cudgels on behalf of the poor Bulgars. This Gladstone did in September 1876 to rapturous acclaim from Liberals around the country. Disraeli's Cabinet split and when, in April 1877, Russia declared war upon Turkey even Queen Victoria was dismayed: "It is not a question of upholding Turkey," she said in direct opposition to Disraeli's policy. "It is a question of Russian or British supremacy in the world."

However, Stead's campaign was not as successful as he imagined. Public opinion suddenly swung from supporting the massacred Bulgarians to fear of Russia gaining the upperhand in eastern Europe – a fear enunciated by the

A 19th Century newsagent in Thirsk with a bill for The Northern Echo *bottom right*

Queen. As Disraeli prepared the fleet for war against Stead's adopted country, events moved in favour of the Conservatives. Russia's financial and military strength had reached a high watermark and she shied away from war with Britain. From a peace conference in Berlin in June 1878, Disraeli was able to emerge triumphant having restored Britain's dominance over Russia in particular and Europe in general.

Yet this too was Disraeli's high watermark. He then embarked upon unpopular imperialist wars in South Africa and Afghanistan which coincided in an economic recession in Britain. Gladstone used the Bulgarian Atrocities and the other wars to highlight Disraeli's moral bankruptcy and in the March 1880 General Election, Liberal government was overwhelmingly restored.

Gladstone wrote to Stead in Darlington, thanking him for his support and encouragement, and told him that it was "a great honour (for Stead) to have been so early and forward in giving expression to the feelings of the nation" during the Bulgarian Atrocities.

Through the power of his pen, Stead had inflamed the working man to take up a cause that did not concern his wages or his conditions of employment, but was centred around those high-faluting concepts of justice and decency. He had showed the power of the press, how newspapers could be "an engine of social reform" and "a means of government".

Fooks described how he did it: "His forte is not so much in hard logic, as in a ready grasp of facts. With the facts before him, conclusions are formed almost simultaneously... The deduction is made, the opinion is formed, almost instanter upon the presentment of the fact, and a ready pen, rushing over folio after folio, presents in little over an hour from its inception, the idea of the writer in a column of leader. There is no hesitation shown – no doubt. The statement is authoritative, didactic, forceful. The style, judged by the very highest literary standards, may not be of the purest, but this is of secondary importance to this literary Vulcan, who beats out his sentences – frequently at white heat – in such clear, sharp, nervous English, that he who runs may read, and can never fail to understand. Mr Stead does not write for the purpose of filling out an allotted space of the leading columns of his journal... He has something to say, and he says it. He is clearly not studying the convictions or prejudices of his reader. The reader must take his chance; and, as Mr Stead would say, in his plain and vigorous Saxon, can like it or lump it. There is a lesson to be taught, a duty to be enforced, a government to be warned, an administrative weakness to be shown up, an evil to be exposed. The readiest means to the end are taken; there is no beating about the bush; the fewest words are employed; point and directness are visible through all that is written."

The Northern Echo's *printing crew in Priestgate circa 1890*

These few words brought Stead great acclaim. The Prime Minister, Gladstone, told him: "It is a sincere regret to me that I cannot read more of the Echo, for to read the Echo is to dispense with the necessity of reading other papers. It is admirably got up in every way – admirably got up."

John Bright, the Liberal reformer, agreed. He called it "an admirably conducted paper...one of the ablest, in point of sheer intellect of all the country papers." He told the House of Commons that it was "the leading paper of the most populous and progressive northern county". The historian EA Freeman went further, describing *The Northern Echo* as "the best paper in Europe". And, in an unprecedented tribute to a provincial English paper, the first session of the United Parliaments of Bulgaria and Eastern Roumelia passed a unanimous vote of thanks to *The Northern Echo* for its service to the Christian cause.

Earl Grey, who'd become his friend during this period and later became Foreign Secretary under Gladstone, was struck by how Stead had managed to do all this from Priestgate, Darlington. The Earl wrote: "Stead amused me to begin with. I found this provincial editor was corresponding with kings and emperors all over the world and receiving letters from statesmen of every nation. This struck me as odd and interesting."

Yet in Darlington, Stead was not happy. He was becoming restless. Now he had walked the national stage, the provincial theatre that was *The Northern Echo* could no longer satisfy him. And *The Northern Echo's* outlook was distinctly provincial.

In his 1879 birthday letter to himself, WT Stead wrote: "The times are hard; Bell is very hard-pinched…I am still as much or rather more bothered by want of space in the Echo."

Although the Echo had invested in a web-printing press that could make 40,000 impressions an hour in March 1877, and despite circulation reaching 14,000 or 15,000 in 1880, Bell was still hampered by his original, principled decision to charge half-a-penny for his paper. This left him little room to invest in either newsprint or wages.

Because of the lack of space, Stead's chances of spreading his wings in print were rare. On February 4, 1880, *The Northern Echo* produced an unusually large eight page issue which gave Stead the opportunity to expand his thoughts over a full page, "Mr Cowen – weathercock or statesmen?" being his chosen subject and Sir Joseph Cowen being the Newcastle newspaper baron and Liberal MP. Stead was famous for his ability to remember any pronouncements by any politician on any subject – it was said that he was "the most dangerous man to politicians in all London" because of this – and his article placed conflicting statements by Cowen beside each other to cause maximum embarrassment. Another three pages in that paper are devoted to thousands of words on a Liberal conference in the Mechanics Institute that was addressed by Joseph Chamberlain.

Bell paid his editor £400pa and Stead also earned £50pa for his contributions to weekly papers in the area and a further £60pa for a weekly column in the London Echo.

In June 1880, Stead was offered £800pa to become assistant editor of the Pall Mall Gazette in London. The Gazette also offered him a national platform. It did not boast a large circulation, but it could boast a big influence. It was the paper of the Liberal inner circle – he had been recommended to the post by leading Liberal politician Chamberlain.

The lures proved too great for Stead. In July 1880, he left *The Northern Echo* for the bright lights of the city.

Once there, he made a tremendous impact which catapulted him to personal fame and notoriety. This stemmed from July 1885 when he launched his Maiden Tribute of Modern Babylon campaign – by now he was editor of the Gazette, having replaced John Morley who had become MP for Newcastle. With a classic salesman's technique, Stead told his readers to avoid the next four issues of the Gazette if they preferred "a fools' paradise of imaginary innocence and purity".

He then began regaling them with the ancient Greek legend of how young men in Athens sacrificed maidens to the Minotaur in the Labyrinth. But that was "a paltry maiden tribute ... This very night in London, and every night, year in and year out, not seven maidens only, but many times seven, will be offered up as the maiden tribute of Modern Babylon...tomorrow they will find themselves within the portals of the maze of London brotheldom.

"Within that labyrinth wander, like lost souls, the vast host of London prostitutes... London's lust annually uses up thousands of women... Let us at least see to it that they assent to their own immolation, and are not unwilling sacrifices procured by force and fraud. That is surely is not too much to ask from the dissolute rich."

Dictating to a relay of three shorthand clerks, sometimes for 24 hours at a time and with wet towels placed across his forehead, he told how he had procured a 13-year-old called Eliza Armstrong for £5 from her mother. A doctor had examined Eliza to make sure her virginity was intact and then she was sent to a London brothel where she was dazed with chloroform (a common practice in brothels) and prepared for use by her first customer.

That first customer was none other than Stead himself, and he spirited Eliza away to France where she was kept, for her own safety, for five weeks while the hubbub raged in London. The Gazette sold out and copies exchanged hands for half-a-crown. The House of Commons quickly passed the Criminal Law Amendment Act which raised the age of consent from 13 years to 16. Stead was feted as a hero.

But he had enemies also. They contrived to make him the first person prosecuted under the new law. Eliza's mother now said she had thought her daughter was being taken away for domestic service and pointed out that Eliza's father had not given his consent to the deal (only after the trial did Stead learn that Eliza's parents had not been married). He had also held Eliza against her will in France for weeks and, however sincere his motives, the poor girl cannot have understood why she had been assaulted with chloroform and been kept prisoner in a foreign country.

Stead was sentenced to nine weeks in prison for abduction. He did three days hard labour before being transferred to a more comfortable cell in Holloway Prison. Each November 10 afterwards, he celebrated his conviction by going to work in his convict's clothes.

The debate has long raged as to whether Stead was a saint or a sensationalist. The Bill that he was supporting was already progressing through Parliament before he performed his stunt of procuring Eliza, a stunt that must have harmed the girl although in later life she said she bore no ill will towards her abductor.

It was a stunt that boosted the sale of the Gazette and it was a stunt that he sold in the most sensational way with headlines like "The confessions of a brothel keeper" and crossheads – a new invention to break up the dense columns of type – like "Strapping girls down".

There are also suggestions that Stead was motivated to move in the seedy world of brothels by his own repressed sexuality. He himself said: "Sex passion...like steam...is the driving force if it is kept within bounds. In excess, it bursts the boiler." Stead felt that he had kept it within bounds, using it to drive his project forward. It was those who abused young virgins who "burst the boiler".

His many supporters agreed, proclaiming him a moral crusader. Stead believed God was his "partner" in the editor's chair, and he urged his readership to "be a Christ" rather than a Christian who subserviently attends church once a week. In the Maiden Tribute of Modern Babylon he had combined his faith with his desire to improve the lot of the common man – although to him, they were one and the same. "The service of man is the service of God," he said.

On a professional level, Stead was the founder of what Matthew Arnold called "new journalism". This took the staid, impenetrable newspapers of the Victorian era into the tabloid age. He used multi-deck headlines, crossheads, illustrations and signed articles, where the reporter and his opinions become an integral part of the reportage of the facts, to enliven his publications. He also invented the interview. The Pall Mall Gazette was the first to see this innovation although Mark Fooks recalled its beginnings on *The Northern Echo*: "On one occasion he (Stead) was noticed at a meeting – his reporter being absent – to be listening to a speech of a Member of Parliament. He is not a shorthand writer. He had only a half sheet of note paper, and filled but one side of it with less than a dozen lines, merely giving the subjects, and their order, upon which the speaker dwelt. Next day he had elaborated a speech of a column and a half entirely from memory.

"That the Pall Mall Gazette has practically introduced the system of 'interviewing' into English journalism, had its inception, there is little doubt, in the extraordinary memory of Mr Stead who, it is well known, has done the leading interviews himself, and from memory. This was the case with General Gordon who was intercepted at Southampton on the eve of what proved to be his last departure from English shores. Not a note, I believe, was taken, or but the merest fragment, at the time of the interview, and Mr Stead on his return to London at midnight dictated with marvellous fidelity to a shorthand writer the very lengthy and intensely interesting communication of the opinions of the Soudan hero which shortly after adorned the pages of the Pall Mall."

WT Stead shortly before the Titanic sank

Stead hadn't practised much "new journalism" at *The Northern Echo*, although he did use bold headings and a headline across two columns for the execution of the West Auckland poisoner, Mary Cotton, and in daring fashion he had described the then Prince of Wales (later Edward VII) as "the fat little man in red". But mainly in Darlington he kept to the old style of few crossheads and few features. This may have been because of his inexperience, or because of the restrictions on space about which he complained.

One thing, though, that he did take from Darlington was his interest in Spiritualism. In Fooks' obituary in 1917, *The Northern Echo* spoke of Stead's "trusted lieutenant" who was a "convinced believer" in Spiritualism and who assisted Stead's conversion in Northgate.

Spiritualism had much to do with Stead's death aboard the Titanic on April 14, 1912, two months after he last visited *The Northern Echo* offices in Priestgate. He was travelling to New York to meet Mrs Wreidt from Chicago, "a famous direct voice medium", whom he hoped to persuade to return with him to England, when the liner hit an iceberg and sank.

Ironically, throughout his career Stead had featured stories about sinking liners and one of the more remarkable tales he told on the Pall Mall Gazette was that of the sole survivor of just such a disaster. His prescient editorial comment on the article was: "This is exactly what might take place if liners are sent to sea short of boats."

This is exactly what happened to him.

7 The search for the new Stead

NEWSPAPERS are living, breathing organisms. WT Stead's departure sucked the lifeblood out of *The Northern Echo*. In the following two-and a-half-decades, its spirit sagged so low that it was a regular caller at death's door.

Stead's departure was not the only blow sustained in 1880. Mark Fooks, his "trusty lieutenant" who had been with it since its very beginnings, left to become a district correspondent, probably specialising in the industry of Cleveland. James Wann, who had been manager of the paper during Stead's reign, also went to London to head an advertising agency.

But John Hyslop Bell was still there, and he set about the search for a new Stead. At first he turned to H Innes (newspapers are too busy recording other people's history to worry about their own and so Innes' first name is lost to posterity). Innes came from the Northern Whig paper in Belfast – a Liberal publication, naturally – and occupied the editor's chair for about 12 months. Then came Joseph Lawton from Liverpool. His period in charge was no longer.

John Marshall, editor 1883-1901

In early 1883, Bell settled upon John Marshall as the reincarnation of Stead. He was a Tynesider steeped in newspapers – he married the daughter of the editor of the Newcastle Chronicle. He first came to work on the Echo "as a writer of special, descriptive and political articles" in 1880 when he left a paper in Durham City.

"For a few years he toured the constituencies of Durham and the North Riding and did valuable work for the Liberal Party as a breezy, racy and thoughtful writer," said his obituary in 1905.

He then went to edit the Tyneside Echo, a halfpenny Liberal evening paper, and greatly assisted the cause of John Morley, Stead's boss at the Pall Mall Gazette who was campaigning to become Newcastle's MP.

With Morley's seat successfully secured, Marshall returned to Priestgate to edit *The Northern Echo*. Like Stead at the time of his appointment, Marshall was the youngest editor in England.

His obituary in the Echo said: "A sound Radical, Mr Marshall had a thorough, not to say profound, grasp of political and social problems. His style as a writer was graceful as well as forceful. He had the happy knack of making things plain and those who did not agree with him acknowledged the force of his logic and the fairness of his method."

However, Marshall had more than just Stead's journalistic legacy to contend with. The Echo had been so vital to the Liberals' cause during the 1870s that the Conservatives reasoned that it had to be stopped – or at least prevented from having things all its own way. In the late 1870s, WA Wooler, a prominent local Tory, had taken on Stead head to head by publishing a weekly paper called The North-Eastern Independent at 13, Priestgate, opposite the Echo. The Independent and another Tory weekly, the Standard, were taken over in December 1880 by a new-formed company called the Northern Counties Constitutional Newspaper Company Limited which bought all Wooler's printing equipment.

The men behind the new company were North-East landowners, like the Fifth Marquess of Londonderry, and William Henry Wilson-Todd who was the Conservative candidate for Darlington in the 1885 General Election. On January 6, 1881, the company closed the Independent and the Standard and printed for the first time the North Star. Named after a famous steam engine, the Star appeared on pink paper and was the first halfpenny daily Conservative paper in the country. It was in direct opposition to the ailing Echo.

Such was the Star's early success that its business backers were encouraged to build a state-of-the-art home for it. Designed by Darlington's most famous architect GG Hoskins, the Star took up residence on the corner of Crown Street and Quebec Street, less than 100 yards from the increasingly dilapidated offices of the Echo. The building was opened on August 11, 1883, by Viscount Castlereagh and a local 'poet' summed up how he hoped the Star would put the Echo in the shade:

In the town of Darlington, great victories have been won,
By a paper bold and true;
For darkness reigned around, no light could then be found,
Things were a dismal hue;
Then soon appeared The Star, 'twas welcomed near and far,
As day succeeding night;
Though numerous were its foes, it feared not to oppose,
In the cause of truth and right:
South Durham felt its power, and Liberals banned the hour
The Star first shot its ray;
The Star has made its way, and proud are we today,

To see our building new;
Yet still we must push on, our task is far from done.
We've an object grand in view;
With Darlington our battlefield, Conservatives will never yield,
And The Star will do its duty.

The North Star quickly threatened to eclipse the Echo as it built up the largest sale of any Conservative and Unionist paper between Leeds and Edinburgh. In fact there was a long running feud between the Star and the Echo over the size of their respective circulations. In 1915, the Echo felt forced to dispute the Star's outlandish claims in print: "Recently we gave an instance of how, two years ago, our contemporary gave their circulation to Advertising Agencies at 200,000 copies per day… We have previously pointed out that this alleged circulation was about three times greater than the capacity of their printing machinery in the time at their disposal."

To fight off the newcomer and its extravagant claims, the Echo had to invest. On July 7, 1883, it countered the Star's expansion into Crown Street by expanding in London. It proudly announced it had taken over the second floor of the "handsome and commodious" premises of 186, Fleet Street, next to St

The North Star's office in Crown Street, Darlington, opened in 1883 and still stands

Dunstan's Church. It boasted that Fleet Street was connected to Priestgate by a SPECIAL PRIVATE WIRE and the peculiar by-line "By Our Private Wire" appeared on as many stories as possible to emphasize the direct and exclusive nature of the Echo's coverage.

In the spring of 1884, to reinforce the Liberals' stable which also included the weekly Darlington and Stockton Times, an evening Echo was published. It looks as if the Evening were something of an accident caused by the war in The Sudan. By mid February, a midday edition of the morning's Echo had evolved updating General Gordon's exploits, usually with information culled from that morning's London newspapers – the Daily Telegraph was a particularly fruitful source. On Tuesday, March 25, an advert appeared in the morning edition of the paper stating that a "special edition" would be published at 2pm and 5pm "and later if necessary".

On March 27, a 5.30pm edition carried a Daily Telegraph telegram from Tamanier headed: "Close of the War". It concluded: "General Graham purposes that after exploring the vicinity everybody shall return to Suakim. There were no casualties on our side. The campaign is over."

The end of the war didn't mean the end of the evening. The following day there was more late breaking news, this time concerning the surprise death of the Duke of Albany, Queen Victoria's son, in France.

The last edition of the evening edition of *The Northern Echo* seems to have been on April 3, but five days later an announcement in the morning paper signalled the launch of The Evening Echo which would carry the first installment of "an interesting story of mining life entitled Below the Surface by William Innes". Serialisations were a staple part of the Evening's diet and it was published at 4.30pm and 6.30pm on weekdays and 3pm on a Saturday.

No copies of The Evening Echo survive at Darlington. The last time the morning paper carried an advert promoting its sister was on Thursday, June 12, 1884. Then all goes quiet. Presumably, after little more than a month of life the Evening died that evening – although the idea was resurrected during the First World War.

In 1887, to bring more money into the operation, John Hyslop Bell relinquished his status as sole proprietor after 17 years and handed over control to a limited company. Sir David Dale was its chairman with Christopher Furness, Sir Alfred Pease, JF Wilson, JB Hodgkin and GW Bartlett along with Bell on its board of directors.

Although the names may not suggest it, the board was an incredibly incestuous affair. Chairman Dale was mourning the death in 1886 of his wife, Ann Backhouse Robson. She was the granddaughter of James Backhouse, the co-founder of the bank on High Row, and she and her husband had lived in James' house, West Lodge. Ann was also the cousin of Edmund Backhouse in whose support during the Henry King Spark days the Echo had been founded, and Dale was in business with Sir Joseph Whitwell Pease, head of the Pease family and one of the Durham 13. Sir Joseph's son, Sir Alfred, was one of the directors on the new board and was about to start a political career which would see him represent York and Cleveland as a Liberal MP from 1885-1902.

Then there was Jonathan Backhouse Hodgkin, a cousin of Dale's late wife and nephew of Edmund Backhouse. Hodgkin's extended family also took in his cousins the Barclays – Barclay's bank took over Backhouse's in 1899 – and he was related by his sister's marriage to Theodore Fry – Darlington's sitting Liberal MP. JB Hodgkin had given up the banking business when he married Mary Anna Pease, grand-daughter of Edward "Father of the Railways" Pease, to devote himself to good Quaker works. He was a close friend of the Reverend Henry Kendall whose advice the young Stead had sought in 1871.

Although a Baptist, George William Bartlett was another close acquaintance of Kendall. Bartlett's father had been headmaster of the first Board School in Darlington for 50 years, and George had started his career as assistant to Mr MacNay, the general manager of the Peases' Stockton to Darlington Railway. He had set himself up in business as a coal merchant in 1870, and the year after getting himself on the board of *The Northern Echo* he became a Liberal town councillor.

Little is known of JF Wilson, but in all probability he was from the Darlington, nonconformist, Liberal tendency and so the only outsider was Furness. Sir Christopher, though, was a wealthy Hartlepool businessman with impeccable Liberal credentials who spread the Liberal word through his interests in newspapers. He part-owned the Northern Daily Mail and in January 1906 bought the North Mail in what is regarded as the last of the politically-motivated newspaper purchases of this highly politicised era.

Readers of *The Northern Echo* got a glimpse of the incestuous nature of the proprietors on August 3, 1888, when an extraordinarily elaborate single page souvenir supplement commemorating the marriage of chairman David Dale came with the paper. Finely illustrated on glossy paper, the souvenir told how Dale's second wife was Miss Milbank, the great-granddaughter of the Duke of Cleveland, whose father Sir Frederick had recently retired as MP for North Yorkshire after 20 years. The supplement informed its readers that Sir Frederick had given the happy couple "a gold dressing case, once the property of George III".

Readers of the North Star were also treated to three full broadsheet columns and thousands of words on the great occasion, but the Star had neither the lavish illustrations nor the sumptuous supplement of the Echo.

Barely were the nuptials over than the board of *The Northern Echo* was hit by a bombshell. In 1889, John Hyslop Bell decided to "sever" ties with the paper he had founded. The Darlington and Stockton Times paid tribute to "a brilliant, experienced and enterprising pressman". "The paper in his hands did splendid work for the party and its achievements acquired fame far beyond its local limits."

Bell went on to become coroner for Stockton, a post he held from 1897 until a year before his death in 1920. In his new role, his most newsworthy event was conducting the inquests into the 138 people killed at the Hartlepools in 1914 by the bombardment from three German battle cruisers.

How the Echo celebrated its chairman's marriage in 1888

Bell, who is buried in West Cemetery in Darlington, was replaced as general manager of the paper by John Harbottle. Originally from Nunthorpe, Harbottle, who was knighted in 1918, came to Darlington as a stockbroker and became the only man to be mayor of his adopted town on five occasions – admittedly, his second spell as mayor in 1913 coincided with the start of the First World War and he retained the position until 1916. Harbottle, too, had impeccable political credentials as he was honorary secretary to both Darlington Liberal Club and Darlington Liberal Association.

John Hyslop Bell, the founder who severed ties in 1889

Quite why Bell "severed" his ties with the Echo is unknown, but his departure was probably linked to turbulence being experienced in the wider Liberal world. As if the Echo didn't have enough trouble in the mid-1880s fighting the Conservatives' North Star on its home patch, the Liberals across the country started squabbling amongst themselves.

The cause was Irish Home Rule which William

Gladstone had espoused in the middle of the December 1885 General Election. In June 1886, Gladstone's Irish Home Bill was rejected by the Commons with 93 Liberals voting against their leader. *The Northern Echo's* party was split asunder – and so was its board of directors and its stable of newspapers as well as the Peases themselves.

The Darlington and Stockton Times had been semi-detached from the Echo since Bell had rescued it from the clutches of Spark in 1878. It was printed in Printing House Square off Bondgate and although its board of directors included David Dale, Sir Joseph Whitwell Pease and James Wilson, there were other people involved. These included Arthur Pease, Sir Joseph's brother, and local businessman John Hardcastle Bowman. In the late 1880s, Arthur Pease and Bowman began gently manoeuvring the DST away from the Echo's line which supported Gladstone. This threw them into conflict with Darlington's sitting MP, Theodore Fry.

It is supposition, but unlike the DST, *The Northern Echo* didn't carry a word on Bell's departure because it would not support the Echo's Gladstonian line whereas to the Unionist DST it was grist to the mill.

The blood on the Priestgate carpet didn't stop there, though. In 1890, Arthur Pease and Bowman mounted a coup and bought out the other Gladstonian directors of the DST. This left the weekly free to steer its own course into Unionist waters and in 1895, Arthur became Darlington's first Unionist MP, unseating Fry – a triumph claimed equally by the Darlington and Stockton Times and the North Star. The Echo now had two rivals to tussle with.

The political split among the Pease family was also marked by a break up of the family business. This would prove terminal – in 1903, Sir Joseph Whitwell Pease was only saved from bankruptcy by his kind Quaker friends at Barclay's Bank and he died a broken man. Although the true extent of his difficulties was never made public, he clearly no longer had either the political clout or the financial muscle to assist the Echo as it slumped into the doldrums, surviving only on handouts from its political allies.

And so the rump of the Peases, having lost the D&S to the Unionists, surrendered the Echo. Sir Christopher Furness was interested in taking it over on his own, but when a local Liberal businessman stepped into the bidding, he stepped away. In 1895, *The Northern Echo* was bought by ED Walker.

The new sole proprietor had been born in 1841 in Brighton where his father had been a coastguard. Walker Senior worked his way around the coast and settled in Redcar where young Edward Daniel supplemented the family's meagre income by working on a farm rather than attending school.

ED Walker joined the North-Eastern Railway Company in Middlesbrough and quickly rose through the ranks until he became chief clerk at North Road Station in Darlington. One of his extra jobs was as District Accountant for the British and Irish Magnetic Telegraph Company, his patch covering 65 stations. In 1870, the private telegraph companies were nationalised (one of the factors that encouraged the Echo's foundation) and Walker was able to walk away with "a substantial pension".

With this money, he took over the lease on the bookstall, news and advertising businesses on NER stations in the Darlington district. He quickly diversified into running the refreshment rooms at North Road, Bank Top, Saltburn and Tebay stations and then spread into a stationer's business and Post Office in Northgate, Darlington.

By 1895, he was known as "the WH Smith of the North", such was the extent of his business operations. Given his distribution network, the Echo probably seemed like an ideal fit for his portfolio. He tried to invest in the paper, introducing some new printing apparatus, enlarging the paper a little and replacing some of the handsetting of pages with the two linotype keyboards – linotype had only been patented by the Americans in 1887 and the Echo was one of the first papers in Britain to pioneer this method of make up which was to dominate the industry for 100 years until the computer age.

But bits and bobs of metal were not enough. Britain was engaged in another war, the Boer War, and the Echo's editor, John Marshall, was resolutely opposed to it. "He wrote strongly and with deep conviction against the South African War," recorded his obituary.

ED Walker, owner 1895-1902

At the start of the war in 1899, a jingoistic mood swept through Britain and when news reached home in the Spring of 1900 that Mafeking had been relieved, there was riotous rejoicing. Opposition to the war was not a popular stance and advertisers began withdrawing their revenue rather than be tainted. However, as the war dragged on for a further two years, public opinion swung behind the Echo's principled stance and the earlier withdrawal of advertising cannot alone account for the predicament the paper found itself in at the dawn of the 20th Century.

Some of the problems can be laid at the door of Liberalism which, under the weight of its various schisms, was a dying political creed that didn't speak to the

ED Walker was known as "the WH Smith of the North" because of his string of newsagent's shops. This one promoting the Echo was in Newgate, Bishop Auckland

ordinary working man. Gladstone had recognised as much as early as 1891 when, at a party conference in Newcastle, he pleaded for more working-class candidates to be put forward. But the leader himself was thwarted because too many of the local Liberal branches were small, nonconformist, middle-class cliques – an exact description of *The Northern Echo's* board before 1895.

And because it was a Liberal paper, the Echo felt beholden to print reams of speeches by Liberal politicians that few people wanted to read. The paper still consisted of only four pages, half of them taken up by advertising, the rest by Liberal-speak.

At the turn of the century, *The Northern Echo* seemed to be dying with the old, paternalistic political creed it had been set up to promote in the Victorian heyday. Just as the Liberal Party missed out on men like Keir Hardie, Ramsay MacDonald and Arthur Henderson, so the Echo was missing out on the generation of lower middle class working men which was benefiting from the 1870 Education Act.

That generation was turning to new newspapers which had learned swiftly at Stead's school of "new journalism", papers like the Daily Mail (1896), the Daily Express (1900) and the Daily Mirror (1903). These were chunky papers, compared to the Echo's meagre four pages. They were financed by actively-sought advertisements which promoted the trendy branded goods that appeared at the start of the age of consumerism. The articles weren't long-winded and boring, they were brief and interesting; they didn't concentrate on Liberal politicians, their emphasis was on personalities, gossip and trivia; they didn't think that pig iron reports were all that was needed, they catered for women as well.

By 1900, the Daily Mail sold just shy of a million copies a day, a circulation figure enhanced by its recent decision to print in Manchester as well as London. In 1898, the Daily Express followed suit, starting a collection of Morning Mail offshoots that were printed in Newcastle, Sunderland, South Shields, Middlesbrough and Stockton. In 1901, this collection was distilled into one North-Eastern paper called the North Mail which was attractively designed and even, shock of shocks, featured news rather than adverts on the front.

These publications shattered the Echo's railway inspired dominance of the morning market and started a new war: the halfpenny national mornings with vast resources versus the halfpenny provincial mornings with provincial resources.

Critics sneered that the Echo was "a gallant little paper" that had had its day and was dying with the Pease dynasty. The Echo, to be fair, was raging against the dying of the light. In 1901 Marshall, the editor, left after a 20 year reign to pursue his "literary interests" in London where he died four years later. John Mason steered the paper over the Christmas and New Year period until in 1902 Thomas Cox Meech arrived and set about making changes. He had edited the London Echo, the first halfpenny evening paper of a Liberal persuasion. On his second day in charge, February 26, he introduced Hear All Sides, a readers' letters column which has survived, bar an uninspired switch to Echo Letters in the mid 1990s, to this day.

The Saturday paper was doubled in size to include Our Weekly Magazine, which was a couple of pages of anecdotes and snippets from national magazines, a chess column and some women's features.

By the end of 1902, the daily paper had acquired an extra two pages. A large cartoon from the Westminster Gazette provided impact on Page 2; Page 4 had a column of local digests called Echoes of the North; Page 5 carried a column called Five O'Clock Tea which dealt in gossip, another column The World of Music and a half-page serialised story.

But was this enough? For not only did the Echo have to contend with the rapidly changing business in the country as a whole, it also had huge problems closer to home. Priestgate needed substantial investment. Cox Meech said the paper was an inefficient concern with modest offices; the editorial and printing departments were either sides of a yard strewn with discarded tin cans. And the press, he said, was "watched anxiously lest the machine should stop if somebody coughed too loudly".

ED Walker had had enough. Officially, he was tired. "Mr Walker had many calls upon his energy", says the Echo's only previous stab at a history in 1917. "For a number of years he was a councillor and alderman of the Darlington Corporation, a member of Durham County Council, a member of the School Board, the Board of Guardians and a Justice of the Peace. He was three times mayor of the Borough, was connected with almost every influential organisation in the north and was knighted in 1908."

Unofficially, Walker had spread himself too thin. Being astute he realised he could do no more with this loss-making relic of a bygone age. He wanted out.

He probably realised that what *The Northern Echo* required if it were to survive was backers with money and influence way beyond those of a backwater businessman. It required someone with vision and energy to re-establish its name and to steer it on a new course. In short, it required a new Stead.

What Walker doesn't seem to have realised was that man had been on his staff since 1897.

A printers' "wayzgoose" - or outing - prepares to leave Priestgate in the early 20th Century for Scarborough

8 The Starmer years

THE new Stead was Starmer, Charles Walter Starmer. He was a businessman not a journalist, but he was inspired by the great writer and campaigner.

In a leader in *The Northern Echo*, Stead had written that the country needed "a series of newspapers...which would give assurance against revolution and give the man in the street who is striving for a better standing of things amongst his fellows the opportunity of explaining the grievances from which they suffer".

Starmer later resolved "that if ever the opportunity came, he would do what he could to help bring about the realisation of Mr Stead's idea".

As ever, Stead was a visionary. It wasn't until after the First World War that four series of newspapers came to dominate the publishing industry. Although they did give a platform for the working man to express his grievances, their formation was more about making money for their owners. Those four groups were Northcliffe Newspapers, Kemsley Newspapers, Provincial Newspapers and Westminster Press. The latter was also known as the Starmer Group because it revolved around *The Northern Echo* in Darlington and Sir Charles in person – he was knighted in 1917 for public services.

But before Starmer could even think about building an empire he had to save the Echo.

He was born in Lincolnshire on July 12, 1870 – six months after the Echo had been born – and had moved with his parents at an early age to Loftus on the Cleveland coast. He left school at the age of 13 and it wasn't until his late twenties that he found his vocation. Early in ED Walker's proprietorship, Starmer was appointed to the Echo's West Hartlepool office at 42, Whitby Street. He may even have been the sole employee at the outpost. His prime duty was as an advertising rep but on his travels collecting accounts he also picked up news snippets.

Just before the turn of the century, Walker brought him to head office. Starmer was shocked by what he found. Priestgate consisted of "a few two storey houses in a state of decay and the production of the paper was achieved by primitive methods indeed".

In 1902, when Walker intimated that he wanted out, it fell to Starmer to put together a rescue package. His motivation, like that of fellow sometime Hartlepudlian Bell, was politics – Starmer was secretary of the Darlington Liberal Association and was elected to the town council in 1903.

He approached the wealthy Rowntree family of York, bastions of Liberalism and chocolate entrepreneurs. Initially he promised the Rowntrees that if they could drum up a page of advertising, he would launch a York edition of the Echo to promote Liberalism in the city.

After negotiations, Joseph Rowntree, head of the family, decided to take over the Echo altogether and on April 1, 1903, he formed the North of England Newspaper Company. His son Arnold became chairman – a post he held for 47 years – and the board consisted of Joseph, John Bowes Morrell and Ernest Parke. Morrell was an active Liberal who was already on the Rowntree board and Parke was recruited for his journalistic experience: he had run the London Liberal papers The Morning Leader and the evening Star.

The takeover, which coincided with fellow chocolate-makers Cadburys acquiring newspaper interests, led to jibes of a "cocoa press". Political opponents claimed that the Rowntrees and the Cadburys were more interested in promoting their businesses than their politics in their papers. Perhaps stung by these jibes, in 1904 Rowntree handed over the North of England Newspaper Company to the Joseph Rowntree Social Service Trust.

Starmer was appointed general manager of the Echo but Parke wanted his own man in the editor's chair. He approached a member of his Morning Leader staff, George Gilbert Armstrong, and asked if he fancied the Darlington job. Armstrong was prime Echo material: his father and both his grandfathers were Unitarian ministers and he was a Liberal activist. Although he was born in Nottingham (on May 22, 1870, a month-and-a-half before Starmer), he had worked for two years in the mid 1890s on The North-Eastern Gazette in Middlesbrough. Indeed, Armstrong had been interviewed for the editor's post in 1902 but Walker had preferred Thomas Cox Meach because "he had written a book".

After several months, Cox Meach was eased out of the editor's chair – he went to London to become London editor, Parliamentary correspondent and for more than 15 years contributed serial stories as well as news copy – and Armstrong, on the substantial salary of £8 per week, took over. He was "appalled" by what he discovered.

"The paper was then small and was printed on green paper and looked very provincial indeed in its make up with small advertisements displayed on the first page," wrote Armstrong in his memoirs which suggests his memory was not always accurate – green paper? "It had been agreed that there must be a revolution, modelling the new paper on The Morning Leader itself with the leading news on the front page and sharing many features with The Leader. That, no doubt, was why Parke wanted a man of his own in the editorial chair."

The revolution on the ground had really begun in October 1903 when

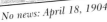

No news: April 18, 1904

News: April 19, 1904

Tyneside's only Liberal newspaper, the Newcastle Daily Leader, had been taken over by the Conservative North Mail. This coincided with the Sunderland Echo moving away from conventional Liberalism and Starmer had seized the opportunity to start a Newcastle edition of the genuinely Liberal Northern Echo. An office, with two staffers, was opened in Newcastle and the most northerly outpost was the Berwick office.

Armstrong started the revolution on the paper on April 19, 1904. Not only did it become larger but news appeared on the front page – Parke's The Star had been the first paper to put news on the front in 1890 but the Echo had only toyed half-heartedly with the idea with stray leader columns rarely cropping up among the advertisements on important occasions (The Times was the last paper to adopt front page news when it changed on May 3, 1966).

To justify the historic change, Armstrong wrote a leader entitled "For Progress. The enlarged Northern Echo and what it stands for".

He said: "Once again, moving with the ever-growing requirements of the times, *The Northern Echo* presents itself to its readers in an enlarged form. It is today the only Liberal morning paper between Bradford and the Tweed. With the steady encroachment of the advertisers, consequent upon a rapidly growing circulation, the eight additional columns of space represented to our readers this morning have become an imperative necessity. All departments of the paper will gain from this enlargement."

Indeed, for the first time, there is mention of sports reporting being important to the Echo.

With an eye to the gathering war clouds, perhaps the most interesting of Armstrong's thousands of words came under the heading of "International Peace": "We stand for international peace – for the substitution of international law and international law courts for the senseless arbitrament of war and we are opposed to insane competition in the piling up of armaments. We stand for the conversion of our soldiers into a unit of an international police force, prepared for the defence of our own shores against invasion." Although this failed to foresee the outbreak of the First World War, it predicted the formation of the League of Nations and only at the turn of the 21st Century is the United Nations grappling with the role of an international police force.

Soothsaying aside, Armstrong insisted that the Echo's primary purpose was unchanged: "But, after all, the mission of *The Northern Echo* is, first and foremost, political. It aims at making itself the best possible all-round newspaper, in order that it may find scope for the work which its proprietors and conductors have set before them of upholding the flag of progress and affording a vehicle for the promulgation of Liberal ideas throughout these northern counties.

"For what, then, do we stand? We stand for the right of every man to the free direction and development of such faculties as God has given him – limited only where that freedom comes in conflict with the rights of his neighbour."

Despite Armstrong's protestations, though, the Echo's days of pushing party politics were numbered. In 1903, shortly before his arrival, there had been a by-election at Barnard Castle in which *The Northern Echo* had for the first time preferred a Labour candidate to a Liberal one. Many factors influenced this controversial switch of allegiance. The Liberal candidate was not a traditional Liberal in that he was not wedded to the principle of free trade, one of the Echo's belovéd causes. The Labour man was Arthur Henderson who had close links to the Echo's heart beyond promoting free trade. He had worked in Darlington as agent for Barnard Castle's newly deceased MP, Joseph Whitwell Pease and was a friend of Starmer. They worked together in the Darlington Temperance Society and, as Henderson said on Starmer's death in 1933, "from 1896 to 1906 we were intimately associated as colleagues on Darlington Borough Council".

The switch of support returned Henderson to Parliament and relegated the Liberal to third place behind a Conservative. Henderson became the first Labour member of a British Cabinet during the First World War coalition Government and is one of the central figures in shaping the Labour Party – he

The directors of North of England Newspapers, 1903: Arnold Rowntree, John Bowes Morrell, Ernest Parke and Charles Starmer. Bottom: Thomas Cox Meech, editor 1902, and GG Armstrong, editor 1903-1908

co-wrote the old Clause IV of the party's constitution which committed it to nationalisation. After this momentary aberration, the Echo returned to its party line. This was partly because the enlarged paper relied heavily on articles culled from The Morning Leader and the Star. On one occasion an irate reader in London complained that the Echo's leader was stolen almost verbatim from the Star. When the Echo reproduced The Morning Leader's cartoons about exploited Chinese labourers in the South African goldmines, the Yorkshire Post bitterly accused its northern rival of printing "scandalous and revolting libels.

Armstrong maintained the individuality of the Echo with articles like the major series that appeared over Christmas 1907 about the "causes and cure of infant mortality in the County of Durham and in Middlesbrough".

With a bigger paper serving a bigger geographical area, a bigger press was required. In 1903, £600 was spent up-grading the old press, which had previously done duty for the Edinburgh Evening News, so it could print an eight-page Echo. In June 1908, another secondhand press was acquired from the Leeds Mercury enabling the Echo to become a ten page publication.

And it all worked. In 1902, the Echo's circulation was 4,450. With Starmer in control of the business, by June 30, 1903, he was able to report that sales had reached 5,566 a day and were rising. With Armstrong in control of the editorial, the paper was able to boast on August 21, 1905: "30,000 – THE DAILY CIRCULATION OF The Northern Echo ALWAYS! EXCEEDS THIS FIGURE!"

But the town of Darlington wasn't big enough for both Starmer and Armstrong. In the eyes of the Rowntrees, Armstrong and Starmer were equals. They co-existed peacefully for more than three years.

In his memoirs, Armstrong recalls: "When I first knew Starmer, he seemed a very quiet, retiring little man, but he seemed gradually to expand. His mayoralty helped, I expect (Starmer was mayor of Darlington in 1907). He gradually got aggressive, and our dual control evidently had begun to irk him.

"At last he struck against it. I had unwittingly played into his hands by forgetting to insert a puff for an advertiser in the news part of the paper. No editor likes to put puffs into the news, but it must be recognised that it is inevitable sometimes.

"He complained to the Board and demanded, on threat of his resignation, to be placed in supreme command, and Parke came down to see me and, with obvious regret, told me I must in future take my orders from Starmer. (I never consider it 'cricket' to weight a demand against a colleague with a threat of resignation, at least before the opponent has a chance to get in a similar threat!)

"Starmer coveted (and took) my room on the first floor in preference to the room he occupied next the general office on the ground floor – giving me an inferior room. At any rate, it became obviously inferior when he had a carpet put down for him in my old room and let me continue with linoleum in my new one!"

Armstrong immediately applied to become editor of the newly-launched northern edition of The Daily News based in Manchester (another branch of the cocoa press as it was controlled by the Cadburys), leaving his home in Southend Avenue, Darlington, in 1908. Although he had been in charge for only four years, his contribution to *The Northern Echo* had been immense. On hearing of his departure John Hyslop Bell, the founder, wrote saying that he had done more than even WT Stead: "This is so sudden – though it is neither the disappearance of a debauchee nor the crisis of a courtship. I am sorry for *The Northern Echo's* sake; for your editorship has eclipsed its former best."

Armstrong's replacement was Luther Worstenholm, a fellow Unitarian and lay preacher, who had worked with him on the commercial side of the North-Eastern Gazette in Middlesbrough. Worstenholm hailed from Derbyshire and had started out as a chemistry teacher in Chesterfield before moving into newspapers at Middlesbrough. He had come to Darlington in 1903 as a sub-editor and for a number of years subsequent to taking over from Armstrong had edited the local weekly papers published in Priestgate.

Worstenholm's appointment heralded the end of *The Northern Echo* as great Liberal mouthpiece. The gradual conversion to more balanced reporting might have had something to do with the January 1910 election in which the paper got its fingers terribly burnt by Ignatius Trebitsch Lincoln.

Lincoln's election as Liberal Member of Parliament for Darlington is probably the most remarkable of the 20th Century's political scandals. He was a fantasist with criminal records in many European countries (he had a worrying habit of stealing gold watches), his personal behaviour can best be described as sleazy (he made love to a married woman and her 21-year-old daughter on a sea voyage to America) and he ended his life as a peace-loving monk in China (at one stage he had 17 disciples following him around the world but they left him when he was discovered in a compromising position with a young nun).

Yet in 1909 Lincoln, a Hungarian Jew, had wormed his way into the heart of the Rowntree empire. He swindled them out of thousands of pounds carousing his way around Europe on the pretence of researching Liberal social policy on the Continent.

At the time of the election, the Rowntrees were blissfully ignorant of their losses and pushed him forward as their candidate for Darlington. *The Northern Echo* gleefully took up his cause, publishing many fantastic tales about his wondrous life in 1909. During the election campaign itself, the Echo noticeably cooled towards the maverick and hinted that the Labour candidate was not so much a socialist as a "progressive" but still Lincoln was elected by a majority of 29 votes.

The 1910 Parliament was the second shortest of the century and a second election followed in the December. Within the 11 months of its life, Lincoln was discredited and slunk away to America where he re-invented himself as a secret double agent during the height of the First World War.

The Northern Echo also reinvented itself as a paper with few political allegiances. Despite the wonderful embarrassment of the Lincoln incident, this switch was largely due to business reasons.

In the run-up to the War, the North Star was floundering and wholly reliant on Conservative donations to keep it going. This led it to adopt a slavishly Tory line and Worstenholm found "illustrations of zealous Tories who had actually given up the Star for the Echo, being alienated by the party spirit revealed".

Worstenholm wrote this in an internal memo on Echo Editorial Policy dated May 10, 1914, in which he analysed the Echo's success over the Star. "The assumption could only be that we have a considerable number of Tory readers. Indeed our

Trebitsch Lincoln,
Darlington MP 1910

success can only be assured by making all classes – commercial and industrial – and all parties – Liberal, Labour and Tory – buy the Echo and respect it. That I feel cannot be attained if we adopt the tone, style and methods of the Liberal agent."

In future, Worstenholm wrote, political stories were not to be given the prominence they had once enjoyed. "I argued that the political should claim only its fair share of attention, and that all other public interest should be well served. It is well known that few party organs are financially successful, and that provincial journals with their limited area of appeal, could not rise to eminence and success without attracting all interests."

He said the "directors do not disapprove of the changes", although his sop to them was his explanation that "the newspaper can best serve the Liberal cause by (1) being informative, (2) concerning itself with principles rather than with party, and (3) in finding and retaining an audience to whom, when elections come, the Liberal candidates and party leaders can speak through carefully condensed reports of their speeches".

As well as grappling with the line where political principles were holding back business development, *The Northern Echo* was struggling to prevent its morals from thwarting extra sales. When the Rowntrees bought the paper in 1903, it employed a Horse Racing Reporter and a tipster; it carried selections and racing adverts. Not only did this contravene traditional Quaker principles which saw gambling as immoral, it also flirted with illegality. Bets could only be placed privately; bookmaking was against the law. Consequently, in 1906 the tipster, his selections and all racing adverts were dropped "and only a minimum Racing Service was retained".

According to another internal memo from 1914, it was soon discovered that circulation was hit. "It has been found over a period that the sale decreased slowly but steadily in the Racing Season, and that some of those who left the Echo for the Star or Mail or Leeds Mercury did not come back again when the Racing season re-started," said the memo.

In 1910, the selections were re-introduced but the tipster and the adverts remained forbidden. "The Echo is giving less space to racing than any provincial newspaper published or sold in the North-East area, and is probably the only newspaper in the provinces which did not use Racing News as a means of seeking an extended sale," said the memo.

Coinciding with the reappearance of the selections was an anti-gambling series. "For instance, articles showing up the certain loss of the better were introduced in connection with the well-known races, and sayings by prominent men against betting were inserted in the Wit and Wisdom column," said the memo.

Luther Worstenholm,
editor 1908-1926

Instead the paper devoted its energies to reporting more serious matters that affected people when they weren't trying to place bets. "In difficult labour questions which constantly arose, one man on the staff devoted his whole time to enquiries on both sides with the result that the Echo has been the first paper consulted daily by such a body as the North-Eastern Railway Conciliation Board," said the memo. "So successful were the efforts of this kind that the Auckland Co-operative Society actually refused to support the new Labour paper which was being floated in 1911 on the ground that they had a representative paper in *The Northern Echo*. Questions such as housing, peace, relations with Germany, education, free trade and temperance received more and more support."

And these editorial policies worked, too. The ten year audit on June 30, 1913, recorded a circulation of 30,197. The paper had acquired a Picture Plant in August 1910 which allowed it to reproduce its own rudimentary photographs and in the preceding decade it had increased its editorial staff from an editor, two sub-editors and eight reporters so that it now had a Parliamentary Sketchwriter, eight sub-editors and 18 reporters stationed at Darlington, Newcastle, Bishop Auckland, York, Middlesbrough, Stockton and Hartlepool.

Ten years earlier, Mr Starmer's advertising department had consisted of seven people; by 1913 there were 15, most sharing the editorial district offices although there were also three in London.

The only failure in this period of great growth was the Northern Weekly Echo. It had started on October 7, 1904, and was supposed to emulate the success of the Newcastle Weekly Chronicle. It was 12 pages of features and news, largely culled from the preceding seven days of the morning paper, plus a few added columns and serialised stories. It failed to attract sufficient advertising, probably because the local market was already saturated, and its last edition appeared on September 29, 1906. It was amalgamated into the South Durham and Auckland Chronicle and its main surviving feature was Our Children's Guild conducted by Uncle Joe – an idea Starmer was later to take out and dust down for the Echo with great effect.

This failure did not deter Starmer. He was already building his empire. His first acquisition had been on the formation of the North of England Newspaper Company in 1903 when he had taken over the South Durham and Auckland Chronicle. He quickly followed it up with The South Durham and Cleveland Mercury and then, in 1905, he used Joseph Rowntree's money to buy the Yorkshire Gazette, a failing Conservative newspaper, and the Malton Gazette. In 1906, he merged the Mercury with the Auckland Chronicle and the Yorkshire Gazette, and he made the Malton Gazette a local edition of the Yorkshire Gazette. In 1909, he bought the Auckland Times and Herald for £500 and in 1914 the Stanley News.

A pattern was beginning to emerge in Starmer's dealings: acquiring and merging papers, combining their staffs (Worstenholm edited the Auckland Chronicle and the Yorkshire Gazette before his elevation to the Echo), and printing them all in Priestgate.

But those were only his local dealings. Starmer also had national ambitions. In 1909 he bought the Sheffield Independent; in 1912 came the Birmingham Gazette and the Sunday Mercury; in 1914, the Lincolnshire Chronicle and the

Derbyshire Courier became stablemates in the "Starmer Group". Most of these were bought with the help of affluent Liberals to bolster the Liberal Government of 1905-16. The outbreak of war curtailed Starmer's expansionist plans on a national scale but it did open up an opportunity closer to home. On September 5, 1914, the Evening Despatch was born to bring the latest First World War news to the readers of the Echo – just as The Evening Echo had carried the news of the Sudan War in 1884. But even that idea wasn't new: in 1875, in Stead's time, *The Northern Echo* had published a one-off evening edition to cover the 50th anniversary celebrations of the Stockton and Darlington Railway.

But Starmer's next achievement, his crowning glory, would, on a bricks-and-mortar level at least, overshadow any of Stead's achievements in Darlington.

9 Priestgate Palace

The King's Head banquet to celebrate the new Priestgate office

AMID cries of "hear, hear" after a sumptuous piece of celebratory knife and forking at the King's Head Hotel in Darlington, Baron Gainford rose to speak to the great and good of South Durham and Cleveland.

"There is a story told of a man who once sold his soul to the devil for money, the devil to meet all his expenditure," he told the 80 guests on Thursday, September 13, 1917. "The man started by buying a very large ranch, and the devil paid the bill; he then went round the world collecting antiques, and the devil met the bill. He then began a newspaper, but only a very short time had elapsed before the devil came and said: 'Here I cannot go on – take your soul back.' (**Laughter.**)"

He was speaking at the formal opening of *The Northern Echo's* handsome new offices in Priestgate, and the North of England Newspaper Company which owned the paper certainly knew how the devil felt.

A decade of ploughing money into the paper seemed to bearing fruit in 1914 when it came close to making a profit for the first time in its 44-year history. Then war broke out. Paper shortages meant newspapers were reduced in size and as consumer goods became scarce, advertising tailed off. Compositors were forced to work by candlelight because of power restrictions and with all mechanical energies devoted to the War Effort, it was difficult to get the Echo's problematic presses repaired.

This must have been particularly galling for the directors because before the assassination of Archduke Franz Ferdinand in Sarajevo, great plans had been afoot.

In 1908, the old thread factory in Priestgate where the paper had been based since 1870 was put up for sale. The directors felt "compelled" to purchase it along with the vacant land beside it on Crown Street. The following year, an extension to house the secondhand Leeds Mercury press was built on some of the vacant land.

Still, though, the offices which had shocked new employees for the last 20 years were intact. Therefore, it was with as much relief as excitement that the 1913 annual report announced a £2,000 order for a brand new press and "we have just signed a contract for £3,000 for a further extension to the office and works upon the remaining portion of the land, which, when complete, will give us respectable frontage as well as the additional room required in both office and works".

Building work even began on the corner plot, but with scaffolding rising high into the Darlington air construction came to a grinding halt in 1914. It wasn't until September 1917 that Priestgate Palace was formally completed.

Focus of the offices switched from the old thread factory to a large door on the corner of Crown Street and Priestgate. The building stretched three sets of

The corner of Priestgate/Crown Street in Darlington before the Echo office was built

January 1916...   *...April 1916...*

windows around into Priestgate where it abutted the thread factory (which wasn't replaced until 1933 although such is the closeness of the match, it is difficult to tell where the extension begins). Around into Crown Street, it stretched four sets of windows where it abutted the modest 1909 extension.

Light filtered into the new entrance lobby through an ornate stained glass window, spelling out *The Northern Echo* (the The for the first time recognised in the paper's title). The reception staff sat behind impressive, bank–like glass screens and the offices throughout the building, in which 200 staff worked, were equipped with fine furniture of polished wood and leather-covered chairs.

It fell to Arnold Rowntree MP, chairman of the directors, to open the palace on September 13. To do so he was presented with a silver key by editor Luther Worstenholm, although the front door was only openable from the inside. Having got inside, Sir Charles Starmer, who had just been knighted, showed him *The Northern Echo's* role of honour for the 73 members of staff who had joined His Majesty's forces – seven of them died; ten were wounded (it is interesting that Starmer conducted this part of the tour because Worstenholm, the host, had just lost his airman son).

After a lengthy spin round the facilities, the guests retired to the King's Head to toast the Press and to be amazed when a photographer took their pictures before the starter had arrived, dashed back to the dark room, and returned to hand round prints of them all before they had finished their dessert.

It was also an occasion to make great speeches, and Arnold Rowntree was never one to miss such an opportunity. "The newspaper should be to the nation what the public square was to the Greek city, a place for meeting and discussing," he said. "A good newspaper expresses the thoughts, wishes, troubles, aspirations, and just complaints of the public.

"And the more one thinks about it the more one feels that representative

...May 1916...   *...December 1916*

government today would be absolutely impossible without the influence of the newspaper."

Of the many figures from the Echo's past who were unable to be present – John Hyslop Bell like ED Walker was not well enough – the absence of WT Stead was the keenest felt. It is believed that he inspected the work in 1913 just a few months before he fatefully set sail aboard the Titanic.

To conjure up Stead's spirit, Rowntree fortuitously had a letter from the great editor about his person from which he quoted: "There is something inexpressibly pathetic in the dumbness of the masses of the people. Touch but a hair of the head of the well-to-do and forthwith you have his indignant protests in the columns of the Times. But the millions who have to suffer the rudest buffets of ill-fortune, the victims of official insolence and the brutality of the better-off, they are as dumb as the horse, which you may scourge to death without it uttering a sound.

"To give utterance to the inarticulate moan of the voiceless is to let light into a dark place; it is almost equivalent to the enfranchisement of a class.

"A newspaper is a daily apostle of fraternity, a messenger who bringeth glad tidings of joy, of a great light that has risen upon those who sit in darkness and the shadow of death."

Rowntree used the Echo Bureau as an example of the great light that was now being shed on the paper's readers. The Bureau was Starmer's idea. It had been billed on Friday, September 10, 1916, as a forthcoming series on war pensions, but over the weekend the idea was fleshed out and it appeared on the Monday as a column entitled Pension Point in which experts answered servicemen's questions about their allowances. On December 16, Pension Point's scope was widened and it was rechristened the Pension Bureau. On November 28, 1917, its scope became wider still to deal with all readers' queries.

Sumptuous Priestgate in 1917: the lobby staircase (left); the general manager's office (top right); the reporters room (centre right); the press (bottom left) and the all-female typists pool (bottom right)

At the opening of Priestgate Palace, Rowntree said that 100 men a week were being helped to receive the pensions to which they were entitled and by the end of the war the Bureau, which had been pooled to other papers within the Starmer Group, was receiving 30,000 letters a year.

Although *The Northern Echo* had sponsored an inventors' competition in 1897 and even earlier Stead had inflamed public opinion with his tub-thumping, the Echo Bureau was the first example of the mass involvement and interaction with readers which was to characterize Starmer's newspaper empire as it continued to expand once peace returned to Europe.

10 Nignogs, profits and pickets

ONCE the gloom of the First World War lifted, *The Northern Echo* emerged into the bright light of the inter-war years full of hope. It was on the threshold of the most successful period in its history populated by Nignogs, Box Brownie cameras, soaring circulation and even, quite startlingly, profit. It is no coincidence that during this period Sir Charles Starmer, the brightest business brain in the paper's entire history, was at the height of his powers.

Charles Starmer when Mayor of Darlington

"With the advent of Starmer, a new type of personality began to dominate the local journalistic scene, an organiser rather than a communicator, a shrewd financier who saw a newspaper had to be a successful business before it could reach a wide audience with its views," said Maurice Milne in his authoritative analysis of North-East newspapers.

Starmer's shrewd influence can be seen in Luther Worstenholm's replacement of the Echo as a paper of moderate political weight in the years leading up to the war – a policy that soon looked sound given that Liberalism was a dying creed in the inter-war years, replaced by Labour, and that the Liberals themselves were hopelessly split throughout the 1920s and 1930s. However, Worstenholm's leaders show that the paper didn't suffer from a cynical business spirit; its soul was still very caring and compassionate.

Immediately war ended, Starmer resumed his buying policy, acquiring the Durham County Advertiser, the Durham Chronicle, the Lancaster Guardian and the Morecambe Guardian in 1919 alone.

Locally, the most significant purchase was the Durham County Advertiser, the North-East's longest extant paper having been founded in 1814 when it was the only paper between Newcastle and York. It had been a virulent Tory newspaper, in bitter confrontation with its rival the Durham Chronicle, but had mellowed in recent years – its editors had included two Anglican clergymen and a woman, Miss Sarah Duncan whose family had owned it.

Starmer now stabled it, along with the Durham Chronicle, with his existing weeklies the Auckland Chronicle and the Stanley News. In 1923 he added the Consett Chronicle to this mini-group within a group, and in 1934 they all formed the Durham County Advertiser Series which was augmented by the Seaham Weekly News (1938) and the Chester-le-Street Chronicle (1940).

Yet the Great War left a tough legacy for the Starmer Group's flagship, *The Northern Echo*. Despite the restrictions upon it, the Echo had fought a good war as the public's appetite for information proved insatiable. Circulation had risen towards 50,000 and, coupled with the Northern Despatch's evening publication, the people of Darlington had had a 24-hour news service. This was despite the Echo's ambivalent attitude towards the conflict which mirrored its difficulties during the Boer War. It hated censorship and conscription and its chairman Arnold Rowntree was a pacifist who insisted the war itself could not be justified.

When the fighting was over, economic depression fell upon the country. For the Echo, rising costs were compounded by a railway strike in 1919. For the first time in 49 years, the country's first halfpenny morning paper was forced to raise its cover price to a full one penny.

The rise proved to be sufficient until after the Second World War, but it wasn't enough for the Joseph Rowntree Social Service Trust which owned the North of England Newspaper Company. It couldn't provide the capital necessary if the Echo were to fight off the cut-throat competition of the aggressive nationals and the pretty pictorials that were springing up all over the place. Indeed, so tough was the climate that the North Star wilted, amalgamating with the Newcastle Journal in January 1924 and surrendering its mock-Gothic building in Darlington.

Anxious to cling to the Liberal papers that were practically all that was left of their political faith, the Rowntrees negotiated the sale of the Echo and its 20 satellite papers to Lord Cowdray. He was the head of the engineers S Pearson and Company which had built the Blackwall Tunnel beneath the Thames in London and the Mexican Grand Canal in South America. Of Liberal persuasion, Cowdray had been one of a syndicate which had bought the Westminster Gazette in 1908. By 1920 he was its sole proprietor and had formed a company with his son, the Honorable Harold Pearson, called Westminster Press Ltd to transform the Gazette, which was losing £20,000 a year, from an evening into a morning paper.

In 1921, Westminster Press bought all the titles owned or co-owned by the Rowntrees. This large group was organised so that smaller subsidiary companies, like North of England Newspapers, controlled the publications in the provinces. But the parent company ruthlessly controlled all that could be centralised – advertising, accounting, buying of equipment, and the pool of London journalists.

Starmer was a hugely influential figure within Westminster Press. He would dash up from London on a Friday night to his home of Danby Lodge off Coniscliffe Road. Bright and early on Saturday morning, he would grill the Echo's department heads about the previous week's business. At 11am he would adjourn to Fox's café in Northgate to play dominoes with his cronies – but this was probably the most important doms school Darlington had ever seen for Starmer and his Greenbank Chapel accomplices controlled the borough council during the 1920s and 1930s. Perhaps their most notable municipal achievement was the building of the Gladstone Street Baths with its revolutionary portable floor which allowed it to transform itself from a swimming pool into a dance hall at the drop of a band leader's baton.

Starmer, though, had wider personal political ambitions beyond Darlington council. In 1918, he offered himself unsuccessfully as Liberal candidate to the people of Sedgefield, but he did make it to the House of Commons as MP for Cleveland in 1923. Unfortunately, a second election was quickly called in 1924 and Starmer was defeated and although he stood again in 1929, Liberalism was in its final death throes and he retired from national politics.

Westminster's loss was Westminster Press' gain, and just as Starmer was hugely influential within the group, so *The Northern Echo* was vitally important to all that he did. He used it as a sounding board for many of his circulation-boosting ideas that, having proved successful in Darlington, were later employed on his papers in Bradford, Sheffield, Nottingham and Birmingham which between them had sales of over a million copies every day.

Many of these ideas now look like gimmickry but their main purpose was to get the readers involved in the newspaper, to make them feel part of one large happy family. Gifts were a good way to buy a reader's loyalty. In January 1920, the Echo celebrated its 50th anniversary by giving away inscribed silverplate teapots to 660 couples celebrating their silver wedding anniversaries; 177 couples celebrating their golden weddings and two celebrating their diamond weddings received silver tea services. The 113 children born on January 1, 1920, were awarded savings certificates and pensioners also received some form of awards.

After 1920, gifts and gimmicks showered from the Echo: books, dictionaries and – best of all as they introduced readers to the photographic age – Box Brownie cameras were given away as was money: *The Northern Echo's* "mystery men toured the district, giving away cash when challenged."

Trains were chartered to take the happy family of Echo readers away on cheap holidays – even a steamship was hired to take the adventurous boating to Belgium. For the 1927 total eclipse which blacked out a swathe of North Yorkshire and South Durham, the Echo hired a plane so that its purple-prosed

The

Northern Echo

The Great North Country Morning Newspaper which is printed several hours later than any London Paper on Sale in the North, and therefore gives

The Latest News.

EVERY

MORNING

ONE

PENNY

penman could take to the skies above its readers' heads to get a closer look – this turned out to be a masterstroke of self-publicity for, as clouds blocked most of the celestial show all the millions of people on the ground could see was the Echo plane buzzing away.

So the newsagents didn't feel left out, those who sold extra copies of the paper received inscribed hairbrushes.

But the best gimmicks of all were those that created mass participation among the readership. During the late 1920s, the Echo treated 12,000 children a day, whose parents were unemployed, to film shows. In 1930, the Big Swim was launched for *The Northern Echo* Trophy. Male entrants swam the Tees from Stockton to the Transporter Bridge. Although the record entry was only 54 in 1933, on July 7, 1934, 20,000 spectators watched the competitors swim the course (the Big Swim was beached soon afterwards when the polluted Tees proved injurious to the swimmers' health).

In-paper, there were coupons to collect and long-running competitions to enter. For example, in late 1929 readers were invited to choose the 12 most eminent people of the era from a list of 30 candidates whose biographies were printed on consecutive days. Plus, of course, there was Echo Bureau which even in 1939 was receiving 10,000 inquiries every year.

There are two gimmicks, though, that stand-out. The first was Reader Insurance. To receive free cover you had to subscribe to the paper, if you missed a day your cover lapsed. And you –

Left: a bookmark given free to readers

or your widow and grieving family if the worst came to the worst – would lose
out on £5 if you broke a jaw at the theatre or cinema; £50 if you died in the
home; £100 if you were killed by "the collapse of any grandstand in any
recognised racecourse or football or recreation ground; and £1,000 if both man
and wife were killed in a train crash".

Imagine the paper's liabilities then when in 1928 there was a terrible crash at
Bank Top station and 25 people were killed. It was Reader Insurance's biggest
pay-out – although it provided good copy. Indeed, it is hard not to wince when
looking back on some of the stories of the 1920s when the Echo trumpeted the
benefits of its insurance. Ghoulishly, any misfortune that befell a subscription
reader was given prominence if the Insurance paid out to his grieving family.

Mysteriously, Reader Insurance itself died a death just as the Second World
War broke out – even the kind-hearted Echo could not recompense all the
families for the tragedies they were about to endure.

The second gimmick of the era that stands out was the Nignog Club. Nig and
Nog were "two little imps who live in the Land of the Moon, their chief
occupation to keep the Man in the Moon awake", and their club started on
Monday, October 21, 1929. It was hosted by Uncle Mac (Derek McCullogh who
also hosted BBC Children's Hour on the wireless) and Uncle Ernest (Ernest
Noble, a Darlington artist who drew the cartoons).

The first young reader was enrolled in the club on November 12; by January
30, 1930, a staggering 50,000 had signed up. Such was the demand in those first
11 weeks that the factory producing enamel Nignog Club badges couldn't keep
pace as pester power swept the North-East.

A Nignog troupe toured the region putting on dance shows in village halls,
raising money to send thousands of unhealthy or poor children to the Cober
Hill guest house near Scarborough.

Royalty now became aware of the Nignogs and Sir Charles himself. On May
5, 1933, in his second term as Darlington mayor, Starmer
presided over the opening of the Darlington Memorial
Hospital. The guest of honour was Prince George, the
Duke of Kent.

The following day, Starmer took George to
Cober Hill where 400 children were convalescing as
guests of the Nignogs and there, on the cliffs
overlooking the North Sea, the Prince was enrolled
as an honorary Nignog.

Perhaps the excitement was all too much for Sir
Charles. A month later, on June 27, he was

Nignog Club Badge

A Nignog Club outing prepares to leave Crown Street in the early 1930s

suddenly taken ill at his London residence in Westminster and died. For not only had Sir Charles been escorting Royalty and presiding over hospitals, he had been attempting to rebuild an entire town. His second term as mayor coincided with a deep economic depression in Darlington, and one of his recurring themes was that the council and local businesses should wherever practical spend money to create jobs for the unemployed. It was a policy that added £300,000 to Darlington's economy, and its pride of place was the extension of the Echo building further into Priestgate.

When Sir Charles died, there were 40 newspapers under his spell and in his later years, once the Westminster Gazette had been disposed of in 1928, the Group had begun to return a modest profit. Even its flagship *The Northern Echo*, which had sailed more stormy seas than most, had turned to a profit-making course: in 1929 its circulation had consistently touched 100,000 for the first time and it is believed that in that same year it returned its first profit in 59 years.

Surely it can't be coincidence that the profit and circulation hitting the magic mark occurred in the year that the Nignogs were launched – a brainchild of Starmer himself. The club, though, was a shortlived success. It quickly expanded from its corner to fill half a page, but when Uncle Mac handed in his farewell letter on October 19, 1936, it was back in a corner and was largely cartoonless as Uncle Ernest had slipped away. On October 24, Uncle David took over the reins, bringing with him the Happyville Times, a new cartoon strip about animals.

But on September 1, 1939, Uncle David suddenly appeared Nignogless with just his Children's Corner. On September 2, Uncle David disappeared altogether leaving no trace of a Children's Corner. On September 3, a Sunday, the Second World War broke out and neither Uncle David nor Nig nor Nog ever returned again.

The success of the Starmer era in which circulation soared from 5,000 in 1903 to 30,000 in 1914 to 100,000 in 1929 cannot simply be put down to shrewd marketing gimmicks and little imps who lived in the moon. Much of the credit must also go to the journalists who, perhaps for the first time in the paper's life, had worked out what it should represent to achieve mass appeal within its patch. This was all the more remarkable given that for much of the 1920s and 1930s the area that it served was deep in depression. Although there are countless stories of long terraced streets down which a single copy of the Echo passed, with each householder paying the 1d cover charge to the previous one, circulation still averaged 90,000 in those two troubled decades.

In 1930, the Echo was described as "very much a locally-orientated paper". It certainly didn't ignore national and international news, but it dug deep into the local concerns of its population and earned for itself the soubriquet "The Miner's Bible". So attached to it were the miners of the Durham coalfield that when they fled the local depression in 1909 to seek work in the newly-opened Thorne Colliery near Doncaster, a special "Doncaster Parcel" was despatched so they shouldn't feel homesick.

Some of the attachment can be explained by the fact that *The Northern Echo*

A wrapper containing a 1907 copy **The Northern Echo** *for a special delivery*

The press in 1934

*First day of the 1926 General Strike
with a typewritten lead story*

was extremely good value for 1d – even if you weren't lavished with a gift or two. For your penny you got 14 to 18 pages which covered local sport, commerce and politics, which specialised in local industry reporting but also offered women's features, a children's club and a goodly smattering of pictures.

The size of the Echo was due to judicious investment in its printing press – an investment which also reaped rewards for its evening sister, the Northern Despatch. In 1926, the Despatch was able to expand from its meagre wartime ration of four pages. It doubled in size and then again in 1939 grew to 16 pages. It widened its area from Darlington into South West Durham and North Yorkshire while still concentrating on young people's activities and plenty of pictures. Consequently, its circulation grew, from 6,000 in 1926 to 30,000 in 1950, with 40,000 people buying its Saturday sporting edition during the football season.

Similarly, the recalcitrant Darlington and Stockton Times benefited when it finally came under the wing of Priestgate in 1934. It was sold by Allied Newspapers to Westminster Press and vacated its premises in Printing House Square in Bondgate. There was much staff hostility to the move, but it made sound financial and mechanical success, especially as unlike many weeklies consumed by the Starmer Group, it was able to keep its own editorial staff and independence which earned it the nickname of "The Dalesman's Bible".

Beyond being good value, The Miner's Bible gained a great deal of its good will during the extraordinary events of the 1926 General Strike. The Strike revolved around the miners who felt the pay gains they had received in 1924 had been cruelly snatched away by the mine owners. In a display of unity, the Trade Unions Congress General Council ordered that all workers should down tools on May 4 – at midnight on May 3, queues formed outside Priestgate of people anxious to get their hands on the first edition of the morning's paper to see if the unthinkable was really going to happen. It did. Four million were on strike.

But during the turbulent nine days of the strike, the Echo never missed an edition, although many looked as if they had been turned out on a typewriter. In fact, a total of two million copies of the four page papers were printed and daily sale did not drop below 150,000.

The Echo never officially took sides in the strike. There were clearly faults with both parties. As Lord Birkenhead, a member of the Conservative Cabinet, said: "It would be possible to say without exaggeration that the miners' leaders were the stupidest men in England if we had not on frequent occasions to meet the owners."

Although never going as far as to condemn the miners, the Echo did feel that the strike was illegitimate and it did unquestioningly reproduce the Conservative Government's propaganda. The queues of people in Priestgate cannot have been left in two minds about the Echo's judgements when they read the first

Building the seamless Priestgate extension in 1933. The construction was part of Sir Charles Starmer's municipal plan to re-flate the local economy by encouraging businesses to embark upon such projects in a time of depression

day's headlines: "Greatest strike in world's history...A national disaster."

Naturally, the strikers were not happy. "In County Durham and Northumberland...in some of the pit towns and villages, aggressive spirits...stopped newsagents from handling newspapers, stole and burnt their supplies, and invented all sorts of devices to blockade *The Northern Echo* vans. Sandbags, carts, wire ropes, railway sleepers, broken glass, sticks and stones were pressed into service," reported the paper.

The ugliest scenes were in Priestgate where police baton charges had to break up the pickets who were trying to prevent the Echo from appearing. Rumours abounded that the Echo was being produced by blacklegs: non-union labour imported to do the work of strikers.

"These statements are absolutely without foundation," stormed the paper's front page leader on May 8. "The position is that all the heads of departments, all the members of the National Union of Journalists, and some members of the printing staff, have no intention of dishonouring a solemn agreement. Their considered judgment, taken in no moment of passion or prejudice, is that they must give their fellow citizens essential news of the gravest industrial crisis in the nation's history.

"As men who believe in liberty they realise that at this time there can be no greater danger than a nation without news; a nation in blinkers; a nation deaf and dumb when it most needs its eyes to see, its ears to hear, its voice to speak."

The Echo claimed that its workforce of volunteers, who had made the cool-headed decision to keep the presses running for the benefit of their fellow man, were working "18 hours a day on a diet of tea and ham sandwiches". Yet much of the workforce was either unskilled or young apprentices, the sort of people who could be persuaded to volunteer.

Nevertheless, it is undeniable that there was a huge demand for the makeshift journal. Although the distribution network was in chaos because of the strike, the Echo travelled by road as far as York, Hull, Northumberland and even Goole and Kirkby Stephen.

"There is no room for doubt about the demand and the need for this essential information," said the Page 1 leader of May 8. "All classes of people, Liberal, Conservative, Socialist, Communist, are clamouring for it every morning. For financial as well as technical and staff reasons, *The Northern Echo* cannot possibly supply everybody. The cost of road transport alone is too heavy. It would be easier and cheaper for us to shut down and to shirk our duty as citizens to citizens."

On May 15, the strike collapsed. In the North-East it rumbled on well into 1927 until the miners eventually agreed to accept pay cuts.

The Northern Echo's *sub-editors room on the second floor of Priestgate in 1934*

Albert Clayton, editor of The Northern Echo *1926-1945*

The Echo's stance during the strike had undoubtedly gained the respect of its readership and had enhanced its reputation as "The Miner's Bible". The Page 1 leader of May 8, 1926, was probably the work of Luther Worstenholm. He had just retired after 18 years in the editor's chair, but stayed on to write leaders. "A feature of Worstenholm's editorship, as of Stead's, was the leading articles, but in contrast with the sweep of Stead's impassioned rhetoric, the Worstenholm leader was a piece of balanced argument, a dispassionate weighing of pros and cons, the outcome of an attitude to life which was at the bottom philosophical rather than political," says AP Duncom in his 1952 book on Westminster Press.

Worstenholm's successor was Albert Clayton, a Starmer protege who was born in Retford, the son of a railway official in 1884. He'd begun with local newspapers on leaving school and his big break had come when he was a staff reporter at the Sheffield Independent which was one of the first acquisitions for the Starmer Group in 1909. In 1915, Starmer promoted Clayton to edit another new purchase, the Derbyshire Courier, and after spells within the Group as leader writer on the Westminster Gazette and editor of the Sheffield Mail, he came to Darlington to replace Worstenholm in 1926.

He edited The Northern Echo until 1945, and the continuity that Worstenholm and Clayton provided – two editors in the second 38 years compared to eight in the first 38 – built a backbone upon which Starmer's entreprenurial skills were able to flourish.

In 1934 *The Northern Echo* was employing 400 people, making a modest profit and selling around 100,000 copies a day from Berwick down to York – beyond its South West Durham heartland, it was the leading paper in Middlesbrough taken by at least a quarter of the population.

Clayton, though, put the impressive success down to another reason. His leader on the occasion of 20,000th issue on May 9, 1934, paid tribute to the readers who had read and bought every issue since 1870: "They are the real heroes: the patient, tolerant souls who disagree with much that we write and go on reading it."

11 Gray days

THE Second World War was declared on a Sunday. It is indicative of *The Northern Echo* of this period that it did not go out of its way to either produce a special edition to mark a truly momentous day or to do something really special on the Monday to underline to its readers exactly what they were facing.

Instead, the Echo of Monday, September 4, 1939, led with the anodyne headline "No lightning blow from Hitler" as if he were some kind of footballer returning from injury, and its reports and analysis of the impending global catastrophe were largely by cable from Westminster Press' centralised pool.

In the safe world of *The Northern Echo*, the ante did not appear to have been upped since the Saturday edition when the world had been officially at peace with itself. Beyond the Echo's national pages, it seemed utterly content to continue with its staple diet of local and regional news. War is declared; not many hurt in the North-East. Yet.

The Echo had never recovered from the death of Sir Charles Starmer in 1933. Westminster Press had revolved around him, and his pivot had been *The Northern Echo*. But immediately he departed the scene, Westminster Press relocated to Fleet Street in London and the Echo gradually allowed itself to be relegated to the regional periphery, neither central nor innovative.

Part of **The Northern Echo's** *fleet of delivery vans in the 1930s*

When Luther Worstenholm, editor at the height of Starmer's powers, had died in 1936, the Darlington and Stockton Times was effusive in its praise: "Mr Worstenholm was a leader writer of exceptional brilliance, and all the papers with which he was connected bore testimony to his broad views and clarity of expression as well as to his economic and political knowledge."

When War was declared, the Echo contented itself with a leader that bears all the hallmarks of being pooled from London. As well-written and stirringly patriotic as the leader is, the Echo appears to have been neither brave nor individual enough to stamp its authority on the calamity that was about to befall a generation of the North-East's sons.

"Come what may, we stand committed to fight for the cause of freedom, individual and national; for the rights of the person against the tyranny of force; for the sanctity of the pledged word against the violation of engagements; for the supremacy of democracy against the onslaught of the "pestilence of Nazi tyranny", says the leader. "Never before has war been entered upon in such conditions.

"For those who have passed this way before to give their consent is the best proof of the real moral force that lies behind the decision. No one who knows what this may mean would willingly release the instruments of war. But no one who has seen the results of the physical brutality done in the name of Nazi-Socialism, who has watched the steady deterioration of confidence among the smaller nations of Europe, who has seen the dastardly perversion of Germany's

A delivery van picking its way through a road-widening scheme in Heighington in the early 1930s

youth carried out under the cloak of national patriotism, who has studied the methods by which Austria fell and Czechoslovakia was trapped and betrayed, can have a single moral doubt that this is a crusade which calls for every effort until not merely is Poland free and Czechoslovakia revived by, as Mr Chamberlain, declared yesterday, "Hitlerism has been destroyed".

"It has been said that the great task of the 20th Century, whether we regard domestic or external, moral or economic needs, is by the organisation of a settled peace the removal of the fear of war and the burden of preparation it entails. That may well come after, our present task is to hold fast to our high faith.

Reginald Gray, editor 1945-1960

"There may be dark days ahead when we may be tempted to compromise with our ideals, but if we do, it were better we should forgo the travail, for all that is worth while would then be lost.

"The grim realities of war have already entered millions of homes. The call to sacrifice has been made already and answered, in part by young and old. Never before has the personal contribution of people of all ages and degree been so widely spread. As we value our homes, our families, our heritage and our country so shall we make that contribution which may enable this solemn task to be accomplished soon."

The Echo's retreat into the region coincided with both the Starmer aftermath and the decline of its editor, Albert Clayton. It has not been recorded quite when his Alzheimer's began to manifest itself, but as the war progressed, so did his illness. Almost by a process of osmosis, Reginald Gray assumed the editorship by dint of the facts that this was wartime and the usual selection procedures for such a highly-prized office could not be entertained and that he had been chief sub-editor since 1923.

In the pre-war world, the chief sub was the focal point of the paper, especially when the editor was ailing. There was no news editor, only a chief reporter in charge of ensuring all diary jobs were covered. When the chief sub arrived at 5.30pm, he found a pile of copy awaiting him along with a set of page plans. There were no news conferences in which the executives could gather with the heads of department and discuss what was going to make tomorrow's headlines. Instead, the chief sub was left on his own to decide what was going where and in what form it should be presented. Page 1, exclusively international news, sorted itself as the wires chattered out the centralised London copy which also dictated the paper's opinion pieces. This left Gray free to concentrate on the local and regional pages.

In 1945, Clayton officially relinquished the Echo editor's role to Gray although he kept his editor-in-chief title, ostensibly overseeing the Darlington and Stockton Times, the myriad other weekly publications and the Northern Despatch. Yet such was the sad extent of his illness that there are stories of tragically embarrassing days when Gray would arrive for work to find Clayton ensconsed in the editor's chair in the belief that he was still running the show.

The poor fellow who, in his heyday in the late 1920s and early 1930s, had once worked closely with Starmer developing the editorial content and organisation of all Westminster Press titles clung to life until January 18, 1949 when he died aged 63 "after a very long illness" at his Darlington home of Abbey Leigh.

During the troubled times of the war, the Echo did have the leadership, though, to develop an elaborate emergency plan whereby if Priestgate were bombed, production would be immediately transferred to the Durham office of its sister papers in the Durham County Advertiser Series. On two Tuesdays in 1941, May 20 and October 21, the Echo was printed outside Priestgate for the first time in its history. Few readers, though, can have noticed the Durham editions as they were identical to the Darlington ones – except that they didn't quite fit on the newsprint: bottom lines were lost and the pages appeared on the paper at a jaunty angle.

The war had two other impacts on the Echo. The first was a direct hit – on the Middlesbrough office in Wilson Street which was destroyed. Quickly, the Echo relocated to 66, Borough Road.

It may be argued that the Echo has never recovered from the second impact: the advance of the monstrous regiment of women. In editorial, management

The bombed Middlesbrough office

and advertising terms, until 1939 it had been a male domain with women kept in their place doing chores like typing and running errands. War changed all that. A September 1941 audit of Echo district offices shows that with men called away to the front there are for the first time a couple of trainee female advertising reps doing jobs that previously would have been filled by men.

In Priestgate, the impact was even more obvious. Miss Laura Loraine had joined the company in the 1920s as a humble assistant in the picture library. The wartime shortage of men meant that she was pressed into service as the Echo's first female journalist, her secondment being to the sub-editors' desk where she remained until her retirement in 1963. It probably came as a shock to the male establishment that Miss Loraine was very reliable and conscientious in her work although she may have lacked the journalist flair on which the men believed they owned the monopoly.

So the Echo limped out of the Second World War with a woman in a position of some influence, with London dictating its opinions and front page decisions, and with an editor who had assumed the chair through an accident of circumstances.

Reggie Gray was, however, the first – and, of the 18 editors who have occupied the position in the first 130 years, the only – who was a born and bred Darlingtonian. He was educated at Bondgate Wesleyan School and Darlington Grammar School where he had been the first editor of the school magazine. For five months after leaving school, he crewed a cargo ship which sailed around Africa and was arrested at gunpoint in French Somaliland for refusing to pay the statutory fare to an Arab gharry driver.

After such excitement, in 1912 he settled on a more sedate career path and became a junior reporter at the Echo. By the time he left to join the Northumberland Fusiliers in 1915, he was acting chief reporter.

He returned once more to Darlington in 1919, this time minus a leg as he had been badly wounded behind Arras in France in April 1917. He had, though, met his wife

A 1940s advertising packet

Edith who was nursing injured soldiers but as deeply and as happily as he loved Edith, it is hard not to believe that deep down to Gray himself this was scant compensation.

After 22 years as chief sub-editor, he assumed the editor's chair and his oft-stated philosophy was that the Echo was "a weekly published daily". In its way and its day this was no bad thing. Nothing was broke, so nothing needed fixing. Readers knew exactly where they stood with *The Northern Echo*. Page 1 was their window on the wider world and then they could settle down to the homely parish pump stuff. Only once did the Echo threaten to rock the boat when, in 1950, it began a campaign against the closed shop union agreement at Durham County Council. This was despite many of its readers having gained their jobs by the agreement.

The crisis passed, largely due to the incredible loyalty that the readership felt for the paper. This had been deliberately fostered by Starmer's gimmicks and the paper's heroics during the 1926 General Strike. Gray continued the reassuring stability of the Worstenholm/Clayton era and his reliance on honest-to-goodness local news only tightened the ties with the local community.

The Echo was the place where the readership looked in times of individual crisis – the Echo Bureau, started by Starmer to provide citizens' advice, still performed a sterling service. Its heyday was 1948 when it handled 28,000 queries: 25 per cent of them involved National Insurance and pension; 20 per cent were landlord versus tenant disputes; ten per cent were worries about Income Tax and the remainder was made up of life's most profound problems like what exactly a best man does at a wedding.

By 1959 the Echo was held in such neighbourly esteem that even though a national printers' strike reduced it to makeshift issues produced by strike-breaking executives, invitations to miners' lodge banner ceremonies still rolled in. Given the militancy of the miners' union in the Durham coalfield, this is a great testimony to the closeness of the Echo to its people. It was one of the family and although it showed signs of betraying the family solidarity, it had to be included in every important gathering.

The readers' loyalty is borne out by the circulation figures. In 1939, it sold 85,198 copies a year; in 1951 it was up to 117,533 and during 1952 it broke the 120,000 mark.

This, though, was the high water mark. A price rise in 1957 from 2d to 3d was too much even for 10,000 loyal followers to countenance and gradually circulation subsided towards 100,000 – nevertheless, still hugely respectable.

Reggie Gray retired on January 1, 1960. Shannan Stevenson, managing director of the North of England Newspaper Company Ltd, said: "The last decade has been just about as eventful as any other in the long history of *The Northern Echo* and during it Mr Gray has never swerved in his absolute and determined conviction that the prosperity of the paper lay in its policy of continuing to give a news service of local and regional news."

He died in 1966 at the age of 71. A personal note by assistant editor Maurice Wedgewood on the bottom of his obituary read: "Mr Gray was a journalist of the old school... Aside from his home, his books and his cricket, what mattered was *The Northern Echo* and what mattered in *The Northern Echo* was the bald news of the day. Presentation and exploitation had little appeal, and the livelier arts of Fleet Street none at all.

"It was typical of his attention to detail that most of the biographical facts of his life were left on record in the office obituary file when he retired."

Those bald biographical facts are still in Reginald Gray's packet in *The Northern Echo's* library. They consist of two painfully thin sheets of typing paper dated January 4, 1960, and beyond the dates of a career that ascended to the top job in regional journalism they betray the humanity behind the remote editor who finished each day promptly at 6pm leaving his chief sub to control the flood from the parish pump.

In the year he left Darlington Grammar School – 1912 – Gray had opened the First XI bowling with his left–arm spinners and topped the batting averages. By all

Mark Barrington-Ward, editor 1960-61

accounts, he wasn't especially talented but he was blessed with the most incredible passion for cricket and its painstaking minutiae. It is no surprise that, still in the prime of his youth with the North-East's idyllic wickets beckoning him, he bitterly resented fate's cruel blow which removed his right leg. He didn't play cricket again for more than a decade until, in 1929, *The Northern Echo* and Northern Despatch Cricket Club was formed. For the next 11 years, he was the company's opening bowler averaging 50 wickets a season with his devilish spinners.

The bald biographical facts in his packet record that his proudest memory was a game against a Green Howards XI in which he took the first four wickets with the first four balls – a tribute, he often said with a true cricketer's modest self-effacement which demands contradiction, to the state of the pitch. The other highlight of his career was against Grange Hill when he took nine wickets for eight runs.

His re-introduction to the game he adored encouraged him to start a weekly column of local cricketing news, signed RG, which was pored over by all players in the region, and even in his advancing years he was to be found as close to the sidescreen at Feethams as possible, watching, noting and providing excellent company.

But perhaps the most telling resumé of his journalistic career came from an exasperated sub-editor who one day exploded in frustration in the newsroom. "Mr Gray," he said, with the greatest respect. "You are splitting hairs with a sledgehammer."

There was no grand vision in the Gray days, no feeling of progress. The Echo was becalmed in the inter-war years, its circulation static at 100,000. Unlike the 1930s when at the height of the Great Depression it had devoted its front page to a daring "manifesto for employment", it set no agendas. It was, as Gray intended, "a weekly published daily", and, like the editor himself, it was obsessed by the journalistic equivalent of a cricket-lover's fascination with the most parochial of statistics.

In 1960, Westminster Press made Mark Barrington-Ward editor. His father had edited The Times but Barrington-Ward Junior's only experience of editing was in Uganda. During his 18 months in the chair, the Echo did not progress – one who was there described his tenure as "brief and uncomprehending" – although it acquired a bizarre fixation with events in Africa.

At the dawn of the Swinging Sixties, *The Northern Echo* was fossilised in the Thirties, an era that had died along with the millions during the Second World War. Not for the first time in its history, it was in danger of becoming a relic from a bygone age.

12 Rocket fuel

Harold Evans, editor 1961-65

SUDDENLY, out of the blue – out of India, even – the distant directors of Westminster Press were presented with an opportunity to be daring in Darlington. The editor's job at the Oxford Mail fell vacant. The best applicant was a green but vivacious 30-year-old from Manchester. He spoke with the flattened vowels of a Northerner and was a Durham University graduate to boot. Clearly, he was unsuitable for the dreaming spires, but if somehow an exchange could be engineered whereby Mark Barrington-Ward, who by happy coincidence was an Oxford alumini and was struggling in the uncultured land of the horny-handed miners, was tempted home, it would open up a chance for the boy wonder in deepest Darlington.

"It was like a game of chess", remembered the boy wonder himself of the circumstances that in 1961 saw him installed as the "temporary custodian of the tradition of *The Northern Echo*".

Harold Evans was born in Manchester in 1928, the son of a steam railway engine driver whose father had been illiterate. To ensure young Harry had the best start in life, his father sent him to college at the age of 14 to learn shorthand and typing. "I wanted to be a journalist from that age," he said. "I was very influenced by Hollywood B-movies where somebody's exposing the villain and getting the girl – that sounded good to me."

At the age of 15 he started as a reporter on the Ashton-under-Lyme Reporter and began rising through the journalistic ranks before taking a break between 1949-52 to read economics and politics at Durham University. He returned to the Manchester Evening News and became deputy editor. He won a scholarship to study journalism at Chicago and Stanford universities and in 1960 won another scholarship to teach journalism in India.

"I was supposedly teaching the Indians how to create democratic journalism, but my time there really helped me when I came back," he said. "I was reading all these newspapers in foreign languages like Hindi. Looking through them was rather like Socrates' 'if you want to know what justice is, define injustice'. I saw what was wrong with them. There was a lack of white space and the type didn't flow. When I came to Darlington fresh from India, these things were very vivid in my mind."

But there was much to learn about Darlington, as well. "Charles Fenby, the editorial director of Westminster Press, taught me about the history of the paper. He was a great admirer of WT Stead and intended to write a biography about him. I also looked into Stead and became quite enthused and so Fenby and I shared this common passion.

"You can't sit in Stead's seat and not have a passion for campaigning journalism. I began drawing on the paper's tradition going back to the Bulgarian Atrocities."

It was a tradition the paper had not touched upon for decades. "The paper was absolutely solid in its attitude to the region which longed for community leadership but its voice had been confined to a not very vigorous editorial page.

"A rocket needs a solid base and *The Northern Echo* was deeply rooted in the region. All I had to do was put some fuel in the engine, and nobody had done that for some time."

The rocket quickly took off. In five-and-a-half dizzy years, Evans embarked upon a series of campaigns which had the Echo talked about in the corridors of a power in a way not seen since Stead's day.

Just as importantly, he also revolutionised the look of the paper, dragging it into the 1960s. In his seminal series of books on newspaper design, Evans was frank to the point of rudeness about the appearance of the Echo he inherited. "The 1961 design was not easy to read; it wasted time and space; there was only rough proportion in news display and none in graphic scaling; and the result

NORTHERN ECHO.

NORTHERN ECHO.

THE NORTHERN ECHO.

THE NORTHERN ECHO

Northern Echo

The Northern Echo

The Northern Echo

The Northern Echo

Titlepieces through the ages: 1 (top): January 1, 1870-September 12, 1877. 2: September 13, 1877-March 10, 1883. 3: March 12, 1883-June 22, 1883. 4: June 23, 1883-December 30, 1897. 5: January 1, 1898-April 18, 1904. 6: April 19, 1904-March 8, 1919. 7: March 10, 1919-June 26, 1965. 8: June 28, 1965, Harold Evans' Clarendon type which has become bigger and bolder

was unredeemingly ugly, he said. "Furthermore, decks (of headline) staggered drunkenly around the page in a way that was hard to follow."

"The philosophy of the redesign was to modernise, to make it immediately eye-catching to the reader without confusing him, balancing the design and the facts," said Maurice Wedgewood, the deputy chief sub in charge of Page 1 when Evans arrived.

The front page point size was increased from seven to eight; headlines on the splash were enlarged, dropped to lower case and neatly – soberly – constrained within regular shapes; pictures were given greater prominence.

Quickly the paper won four national design awards to go with the one it had accumulated in the late 1950s.

The wind of change and modernisation blew most visibly through the titlepiece at the top of the front page. It was a historic-looking script, little changed from 1870, which didn't fit in with the new era.

"It wasn't a very good grot," said Evans. "I wanted something that expressed the vigour and bluntness and direction of the region, that captured the spirit of people I'd met like Sid Chaplin (writer) and Norman Cornish (artist). I didn't want to be footling around with a fancy Gothic type."

In his design book he said: "Its antique quality did not express what we hoped was the surging spirit of the newspaper and the region it served; and the directors of the Westminster Press were prepared to agree to the extent of abolishing the 'earpieces' (the tiny adverts on either side of the newspaper's title) which had brought in £2,000 a year.

"There was one additional gain from the new logotype designed by Bert Hackett: it saved in depth one-eighth of an inch across eight columns, thereby producing a valuable extra inch for news."

On Monday, June 28, 1965, *The Northern Echo* appeared with the Clarendon titlepiece which, enlarged slightly in the late 1990s, is carrying its name into the 21st Century.

As well as redesigning the appearance of the front page, Evans redesigned its content. He opened it up to North-East stories – when they were strong enough. Inside, he introduced four editions to make the news more relevant to local people and he made photographs an integral part of the paper's presentation. Midday conference – an innovation in itself – thought out one photo possibility for each edition area and photographers were despatched to get the picture. This sometimes wasn't as easy as it might sound: the most notorious assignment Evans gave his photographers was to capture the Teesside smell which had regularly wafted over him as he gardened in his home on Coniscliffe Road. Even to Evans' surprise, photographer Ossie Stanford succeeded. In Stockton, he came across the mist which usually accompanied the smell and took a picture of it. He returned five minutes later to the same spot and the mist and smell were gone – so he took another picture of the same view. Hence the smell was captured.

"Harold promised that he would give £5 to any photographer who could photograph the smell, and that was a lot of money in those days," remembered the chief photographer of the time, Charlie Westberg. "But Ossie never got his money."

The news pages under Evans also kicked up a stink of their own as they became the home of a "news focus" series of features which explored at depth and commented upon North-East issues.

It fitted entirely with Evans' philosophy of regionalisation that the use of copy and editorials pooled from London should be reduced – but not undermined or eradicated. "I wanted people to be able to take the Echo alone and not need a national as well," explained Evans. "I only accepted a handful of editorials from London. We took a line slightly closer to the Labour Party than London might occasionally have wanted it but it would be wrong to portray Pearson as a commercially uxorious or politically ideological company. Its view was that what was good for the North-East was good for the paper, and that was my view, too."

In his design book, Evans said: "The leader page is where the voice of a regional newspaper should speak clearly and authoritatively for the region. Instead the old Northern Echo led with theatre and cinema ads filled out, when these fell short, with crudely designed house advertising and even on occasion an undertaker's 'tombstone' which completed the funereal appearance."

There was room on the new-look leader page for a new column called John North. John North had been a regular by-line in the Echo during the 1950s when the paper shied away from using real reporters' names, but under Evans Mr North was employed as a gossipy diarist drawing on people and events in the North-East.

(Since 1961, John North has been a regular feature of *The Northern Echo*. For the record, after Stanley Hurwitz started it, it has been written by Les Freeman, Bill Campbell, Jim Wilson, Mike Amos, John Simpkins, Bill Hearld and Stephen Brenkley. Mr North took to the picket line during the Great Strike of 1977 and so did not appear and he was briefly redundanced during a troubled period in the mid 1990s. However, like so many who were sacked in those unhappy times he was soon re-employed, this time as a weekly column under the auspices of Amos once again.)

This should not give the impression that the Echo solely concentrated on the North-East. The early 1960s had its fair share of international incidents which demanded the paper's undivided attention: the Cuban Missile Crisis, the erection of the Berlin Wall and, most famously, the assassination of JF Kennedy. It is always said that everyone can remember where they were and what they were doing when they heard the news of how JFK's vast promise was cruelly curtailed. Harold Evans heard the news on the car radio when he was dressed up in his finery, bow tie and tails, heading for the Teesside Press Ball. He ordered that his driver turn around and return to Priestgate where he presided over the production of a four page supplement that was as good as anything that the nationals came up with.

Beyond shaking the paper so far into the 1960s that most of his ideas were still very evident in the late 1970s, Evans revived the Echo's proud tradition of campaigning. He campaigned against inflammable nightclothes after a series of accidents in which women suffered terrible injuries when their nightdresses caught fire; he campaigned for safer cars for the disabled; he campaigned against the Teesside smell and, although fairly frivolous, it did help clean up the environment; he campaigned – as all his successors have – against dangerous roads, and he campaigned against the prices charged by Darlington greengrocers. ("That started when my wife complained that they were more expensive than in Manchester," he said. "I'm not sure we got it right, but I hope I gave them a proper reply." A delegation of irate vegetable-men occupying his office, threatening to turn his brains to cabbage, probably assisted in them getting a fair crack of the whip.)

He championed the cause of the North-East, vigorously attacking the notion held in distant Whitehall that the people of the region were "a bunch of troglodytes clinging to a sooty past while crying for subsidy". His Industrial Editor Don Evans wrote a major series of articles entitled They Came North to Success which lured further companies north to varying degrees of success.

He championed the cause of Durham Cathedral by organising a son et lumiére which raised enough money for the World Heritage Site to install permanent floodlighting.

"I regard that as a lasting memorial," he said.

The campaign of which he was most proud was forcing the Government to trial free smear tests for cervical cancer for women in the North-East. "I read a paragraph, no more than four lines, in the Sunday Times saying that Vancouver was trialling this smear, and I thought 'why Vancouver, why not Darlington or Newcastle?'," he said. "So I sent Ken Cooper, a graduate trainee, for six weeks to Vancouver to find out all he could about this project. When I look back I must have been crazy as we could ill afford to lose anyone from the newsroom and when he came back he said the leading authority on cervical cancer was living

The Evening Despatch newsroom in 1962 – Priestgate was a labyrinth of rooms and corridors

just up the road from Darlington, a doctor called Stanley Way who was crying in the wilderness at Gateshead Hospital."

With Way on board, Jeremy Bray the Middlesbrough MP was enlisted to ask questions in the House of Commons. Health Minister Enoch Powell initially rebuffed the proposal but Evans persevered and when Bray rose to ask the same question of Powell's successor, Anthony Barber, the reply was positive and the trial began.

"The first thing I did when I got to the Sunday Times in 1966 was write a front page article for the second section about the scheme and got it extended to the whole country," he said.

The cervical cancer screening programme might have been Evans' personal highlight but in Priestgate, his most famous campaign involved Timothy Evans.

Timothy John Evans, a simpleton, had been hanged in 1950 for strangling his young baby daughter Geraldine in the first floor flat of 10, Rillington Place, Notting Hill London. Evans' wife, Beryl, had also been found dead, strangled.

Timothy Evans had confessed to the crime during police questioning although during his trial it looked as if he were trying to shift the blame by saying that the man who lived beneath him in Rillington Place, John Christie, was guilty.

Three years after Timothy Evans had been executed, a new tenant had moved into the ground floor flat and discovered the bodies of three women behind a false wall. Beneath the floorboards was the body of Christie's wife.

After his arrest, Christie admitted to the murder of Beryl Evans but this was regarded as unreliable and untrue, only made "to help his defence of insanity". Christie, too, was hanged, and then the broadcaster Ludovic Kennedy wrote a book about the murders which provided evidence which exonerated Timothy Evans. However, the wrongful execution of a not particularly bright man for a heinous crime did not attract much attention outside liberal circles.

But moving in those circles was Darlington industrialist Herbert Wolfe. "He'd come to this country after the war with only a shilling to his name and had done very well for himself selling chemicals – usually buying them from one department of ICI and selling them on at an inflated price to another department of ICI before he went into making chemicals himself," recalled Evans the editor. "He was also a painter and I still have one of his works, Model Place, Darlington, on my wall in New York.

"I knew Ludovic Kennedy and had read vaguely about the Evans case, but Wolfe sent me a single-spaced article on fullscape which I couldn't bear to read. He kept persevering with me and so I stuffed it into a briefcase when I went to London to meet the directors of Westminster Press. When I read the article on the train, I was so overcome by the feeling that Evans could not have done this that I wanted to pull the communication chain and get off and start investigating there and then."

The fire of indignation was lit. Or was it sparked by accident? Another version of how the Echo came to take up the Timothy Evans case starts with the same impenetrable article from Wolfe which despite all his telephone calls seemed destined to moulder with so many unsolicited freelance contributions in the Features Editor's "many thanks/polite refusal" tray.

"It was an accident," said one who was there the night the Wolfe article finally went to press. "The article was lying around, there was a hole on the leader page, and bingo, the two went together. Then Wolfe ordered extra copies of the paper to send to MPs and Harold Evans realised there was something in it.

"Whereas Wolfe was burning with injustice, for Evans it was more of a journalistic enterprise. He accepted there was a wrong there that needed to be righted."

In March 1965, the Echo began its Man On Our Conscience campaign. The premise was simple: Timothy Evans was a remarkably ordinary man who had been wrongfully hanged. If British justice was this flawed, such a fate could be lurking around the corner for any Englishman.

The logo - itself an innovation - for the Inquiry showing 10 Rillington Place and Timothy Evans

A new inquiry was ordered into the Evans case within six months of the Echo starting its campaign, but after that initial spin of hope, the wheels of justice ground exceedingly slowly. "We had the Man On Our Consciences logo on the front page every day," said Evans. "I remember one executive saying to me after 11 months that we weren't getting anywhere and couldn't we take it off the front?

"I had an ache in my heart about whether I was wasting my time on Timothy Evans, but I said no. There's a saying in journalism that the moment a newspaper editor tires of his campaign is the moment the public is beginning to notice it."

In October 1966, the Brabin Inquiry concluded that it was impossible to establish the truth beyond doubt after 16 years, but it did concede that it was more probable than not that Evans had not killed his daughter – the crime for which he had died. But to balance this out, and perhaps to save the reputation of British justice which the Home Office mandarins did not want to see portrayed as hanging innocent men, the Inquiry said that the probability was that Evans had killed his wife. This was despite Christie's confession and despite the evidence that Beryl had been strangled, as all Christie's victims had been.

"I became enormously angry at the obscurantism and lies that were being told," said Evans, still angry after all those years. "I could see the hands of Whitehall all over it and I regarded them with animosity for screwing the North-East.

"The inquiry said he had murdered his wife but not his baby. It was a typical attempt by Whitehall at a judicial whitewash."

Roy Jenkins, "the best Home Secretary we've ever had" according to Evans, was in a difficult position. He could pardon Timothy Evans for the murder of his daughter, but how would it play if he pardoned a man suspected by the Inquiry of murdering his wife? And what questions would a pardon raise about the supposed infallibility of British justice? Newspapers were already talking about a new-fangled phrase, "a miscarriage of justice" – what damage would giving credence to that phrase do?

Bravely, on October 18, 1966, Jenkins announced to the House of Commons that on his advice the Queen had granted a free pardon to Timothy John Evans. Harold Evans congratulated the Home Secretary for "bringing an honourable end to a uniquely miserable story".

The Echo's editorial said: "Justice is something which affects us all. None of us can afford to be complacent about injustice. If one man can be convicted and punished for a murder he did not commit, so can another. It is not something remote. Once the possibility is there, it could happen to any one of us. This is why, although the case of Timothy John Evans finally ended yesterday with the free pardon, the lesson does not end there."

Rather like WT Stead's Maiden Tribute of Modern Babylon campaign of 1885,

End of the Timothy Evans campaign

extravagant claims have been made about the importance of the Timothy Evans campaign. Stead's campaign coincided with a movement that forced Parliament to lower the age of consent; Evans' campaign coincided with a movement that forced Parliament to outlaw in practice the death sentence – it was removed from the statute book for all but high treason and arson in Her Majesty's dockyard in 1965.

The Echo's editorial of October 19, 1966, concluded with a nod to what had been achieved and a hard glance at what still needed to be done. "Mr Jenkins was right to imply that with the abolition of capital punishment the Evans case could have no successor," it said. "But we must see to it that it is made harder to convict any man wrongly, whatever the punishment."

Whatever its law-changing merits, the Evans' campaign certainly renewed the Echo's reputation as the country's foremost regional campaigning newspaper. Said Harold Evans: "The Sheffield Telegraph had just exposed the Rhino Whip Case where police officers were taking a rhinoceros whip to suspects, so it would be wrong to think that there hadn't been investigations by newspapers previously. But I don't think there had been a newspaper for a considerable time in the provinces that had gone in for campaigning and investigating and persevering. We persevered until we won.

1961-1965: the changes Harold Evans made to the front page of The Northern Echo

"It is very important in campaigning that you make sure that you are right and that you have investigated a solid case. Equally important is that if something comes along that shows you are wrong, you get off it at once. A campaign has to be propelled by honesty and fairness."

With the Echo revitalising its reputation, the spotlight fell on its editor. It was a spotlight Harold Evans relished.

"Evans undoubtedly had an eye for the main chance," said one who was there. "He was always aware of number one. He was often away from the office promoting the paper and, of course, himself."

When he saw off the challenge of Frank Staniford, the editor of the Darlington and Stockton Times and the Northern Despatch, in a showdown about how much he was allowed to pay leading members of *The Northern Echo's* editorial team – "we were doing very well and I wanted to keep various people while still be economical" – Evans was made editor-in-chief of North of England Newspapers in 1963. With his position in Priestgate unchallenged, he set about taking on the world. He visited Malaya and Korea teaching journalism and toured the United States, advising Gannett Newspapers on its growing media empire (hopefully Gannett remembers what he advised because as the Echo celebrates its 130th anniversary, the American company has just become its proud owner).

Most eye-catching of all Evans' exploits was as the presenter of the television

Harold Evans (right) receives the 1963 Newspaper Design Award – before he changed "the grot"

programme What the Papers Say. "It was tremendous publicity for the paper," said Evans. "I knew the Granada people in Manchester who made the programme as I'd been there when it had become the first commercial station in 1956.

"I did a trial in Stockton with Jeremy Isaacs in which I did a piece about Bill Rodgers, the local MP, and they liked it and offered me more work.

"I got £40 a show, which helped, and I wrote the scripts. Charles Fenby objected to this because I could at times be highly critical of the press and I spent time doing it – about half a day a week. I appealed over his head to the board of Westminster Press. The Duke of Atholl and Pat Gibson, the chairman, came up to Darlington to see me when I was in Manchester doing the show. By the time I returned, Mr Fenby had been overturned. They thought it was splendid."

Harold Evans, media star, was being talked about in national circles. "Denis Hamilton, the editor of the Sunday Times, kept asking who was the brightest editor in the provinces and my name kept getting mentioned," said Evans. "I was on the National Council for the Training of Journalists with him, had just written a book entitled The Active Newsroom and I was doing great damage to his old paper, the Newcastle Journal, as we were taking readers off them.

"He asked me to come down to London and become his chief assistant and see if I could swim in national waters."

It was inevitable. Looking back, some in Darlington felt that by late 1965, Harold Evans had done all he had wanted to do with *The Northern Echo*.

"I wouldn't have had a clue what I would have done if I had stayed," he said. "I would just have continued doing what I was doing.

"But I was loathe to leave. I loved Darlington as a town. I liked the sense of community and I loved working with my very professional colleagues.

"We had a lovely house in Coniscliffe Road. Enid was working as a teacher and I had three children, one of whom was born in Darlington, who were happily in schools, and I just wanted to stay. I was in no hurry to come to what I regarded as the evil city of London.

"But the Sunday Times was a very glittering paper, without doubt the best paper in the country at the time. I asked Hamilton for another year or two in the North-East but he said he was thinking of moving on and he wanted young people around him and I had to come there and then."

Evans was clearly aware what was afoot at the Sunday Times. Within four months of his arrival, he was made managing editor of the paper as Hamilton and the Sunday Times' owner, Lord Thomson, looked first at a merger with Westminster Press and then deciding to strike out on their own, buying the Times for £2m. Hamilton became editor-in-chief of the new acquisition, leaving Evans to edit the Sunday. Evans held that position until 1981 during a time in which the paper was bold and controversial – perhaps too bold and controversial because Evans was regularly lampooned in the satirical magazine Private Eye for taking himself too seriously (at *The Northern Echo*, Evans had not been too controversial for libel damages during his era amounted to just a set of encyclopaedias and £90 removal expenses for a colliery overman who had been identified as a strike-breaker).

In February 1981, Rupert Murdoch bought Times Newspapers Limited and the following month installed Evans as editor of the daily paper. He redesigned it, and immediately clocked up its highest ever sale of 526,000. His relationship with Murdoch soon soured and after a bitter falling out he resigned in March 1982 and headed for the US with his second wife, Tina Brown, who was 25 years his junior. While Tina turned around Vanity Fair magazine, he became editor of Condé Nast Traveler magazine and then president of Random House Publishing, the largest publisher of general interest books in the US. He was also editorial director of Mort Zuckerman's extensive media group, which included the New York Daily Press, and just as this book was being written he published the fruits of ten years of labour: The American Century, a well-received history of America in the 20th Century.

"I have a picture of WT Stead at home in New York and a framed copy of the first edition of *The Northern Echo* with adverts on the front," he said. "I occasionally open the frame and have a look at the country's first halfpenny daily. It was just to the right of my eye as I was writing The American Century."

He clearly retained a deep affection for his days in Darlington. In 1999, when Tina launched talk magazine, he was reportedly to be found in deep conversation at the bar. The first edition of the magazine contained Hillary Clinton's first interview in which she spoke of her feelings about her husband's infidelities; other guests at the launch party included Demi Moore, Hugh Grant, Liz Hurley, Henry Kissinger, Madonna, Rupert Everett, Robert de Niro, Salman Rushdie. But, at the bar, Harry held court about the great sub-editors he had worked with on *The Northern Echo*.

"Frank Peters, the chief sub, and Maurice Wedgewood were really phenomenal," he said. "They regarded it as a mortal sin to let through a wrong syllable. They were suspicious of me at the start, but to me the subs room is where the paper, where any paper, really comes alive.

"It was a better paper when I left it. It was more more locally focused and it was doing something for the region. The staff were incredible to work with and the people of the region were proud of their paper."

Perhaps Harold Evans just got lucky at *The Northern Echo*. He took over a moribund institution which, although selling very well and performing profitably, was stuck in a timewarp. It was a blank canvas for him to sketch his ideas upon and then a fortuitously talented staff – "Colin Theakston," he reeled out another name, "he was a truly world class photographer" – put them into practice while he dashed off to a TV studio to revel in the glory. He arrived just at the time that a new mood was sweeping the North-East as the Swinging Sixties got under way: there were new jobs, new buildings, new artistic endeavour, and he was lucky enough to be in the right place at the right time to ride on the coat-tails.

No. *The Northern Echo* was extremely lucky to have him, albeit for just five-and-a-half years. Indeed, the North-East was extremely lucky to have him arguing its case. When he left in 1966, the paper employed 537 people with 115 scattered around its branch offices serving the entire region. And sales of what in 1961 had been a moribund institution had soared by 14,000 to 114,000.

On his departure, the managing director of North of England Newspapers, Shannan Stevenson, said: "Harold Evans was just the right sort of chap to enter the arena, and he went into action immediately with exciting – and at times alarming – speed, and in due course there emerged a rejuvenated and modernised Echo."

Rocket fuel indeed.

13 Strife and strikes

H AROLD Evans' energy and enthusiasm propelled the rocket that is *The Northern Echo* into the 1970s. It continued to win awards: 1974, when it won the best-designed regional morning newspaper category in the Newspaper Design Awards, was the third time in four years it had featured among the placings.

More significantly, even after a price increase from 5d to 7d on October 31, 1970, its circulation continued to soar. When Evans left, about 114,000 copies were sold every day making it the third largest regional morning paper in the country; by 1971, it was selling 121,000 and for two-and-a-half years, it overtook the Yorkshire Post to become the largest regional morning paper in the country.

Crowds greet Princess Anne on her visit to Priestgate to celebrate the paper's century in 1970

That, after decimalisation, the country's first halfpenny daily cost 4p and was considerably cheaper than its rivals certainly helped.

A measure of the Echo's dominance is that in May 1971 it had a readership of 280,000 in Durham and North Yorkshire; its nearest competitor was the Daily Mirror on 119,000. *The Northern Echo* accounted for 62 per cent of all morning newspapers sold in its heartland; the Mirror for 26 per cent.

The new man commanding the rocket was another Evans: James Donald – JDE on official documents; Don to his friends and colleagues. He had started in newspapers in 1943 in High Wycombe and moved to Durham to become chief reporter of *The Northern Echo* in 1950.

Don Evans was Harold Evans' annointed successor. Harry had brought him to head office in 1961 as industrial correspondent and then promoted him in 1965 to Industrial Editor.

It was under Don Evans' command that the Echo celebrated its 100th birthday on January 1, 1970. Free with the 31,054th issue of the paper came a facsimile of issue No 1, and there was a front page promise that in future there would be more colour in the paper which had hardly moved on from the 1930s when it first acquired spot colour. The optimism was as a result of the installation in October 1968 of a new press which was starting to work alongside one which dated from 1948. Now a 24 page broadsheet paper could be printed at the rate of 50,000 copies an hour. The promise of greater colour was fulfilled: at the end of 1970 the Echo was able to boast full colour pictures and adverts.

The 31,054th issue also promised that "from today, we double the amount of space given to TV and radio programmes to increase your enjoyment of these home entertainments". Now on page two there were two wide columns giving listings for BBC1 (transmitting on channel five), Border (channel 32), Tyne Tees (channel eight), BBC2 (channels 51 and 64), plus Radios 1,2,3,4 and Radio Durham.

To celebrate its birthday, the Echo granted £3,000 to found five annual research scholarships pertinent to the North-East at either Durham or Newcastle universities: subjects subsequently studied included religion in the region 200 years ago, the affect of the Roman Conquest on the North-East and housing in Newcastle, 1800-1914.

Yet one doesn't have to be an academic to realise that despite *The Northern*

Echo's outward appearance of contentment and soaring circulation, inside it was far from at ease with itself. The appointment of Don Evans as editor was not universally popular: his assistant editor, David Spark, soon left for London and his deputy editor, Maurice Wedgewood, voluntarily relinquished control of the design of the paper and immersed himself in writing and reviewing.

Changes are natural under a new editor and it would be wrong to point the finger at Evans for any of the furies that were about to unleash themselves. British industry as a whole was on the brink of a traumatic decade of strife and unrest as the nature and focus of business changed. Westminster Press was typical of the old style paternalistic companies run by established families that were about to go through the wringer as trades unions flexed their muscles with devastating effect. Ultimately owned by the Pearson family, WP was but a dot in global picture that embraced American bankers, Californian peanut growers, Royal Doulton china makers and Longman publishers. WP was a part of Longman, as was the Financial Times and Penguin and Ladybird books. Way down the feeding chain was tiny North of England Newspapers.

And it probably felt even further away from the seat of power if you were sat in *The Northern Echo's* Hartlepool office with no toilet, or in the Durham office without a fire escape or on a pile of newspapers because

Don Evans soon after becoming editor

there were only two chairs in the Bishop Auckland office. In fact, Bishop must have felt like the remotest outpost of this vast empire as the rear wall ran wet when it rained and the windows were 'double-glazed' with sheets of polythene after those who worked inside complained about the cold. So advanced was the Bishop office in Newgate Street that in the late 1960s it was connected to the outside world by just one phone. There were several recorded incidents of fights breaking out between journalists, desperate to phone their copy across, and ad-reps, desperate to phone their copy across, as they leapt from their piles of papers the moment the phone became vacant.

Head office was a little better. It had chairs and worktops for four reporters. But there were eight of them. And only one phone. Downstairs in tele-ads, "dust hung from the ceiling like grapes". So outraged was one tele-ad girl that she persuaded a photographer to take pictures of the filth and sent them to WP's head office. The office was then redecorated.

Elsewhere, unions dominated the workplace. The printers and process workers operated a closed shop – you had to be a member of either the National Graphical Association (NGA) or the Society of Lithographic Artists, Designers, Engravers and Process Workers (SLADE) to get a job. It also seemed as if the workers themselves operated a closed shop – you had to be a member of certain families before you could get a job down the Echo.

There was strict demarcation of duties – if a journalist or advertising rep dared to overstep in the printers' domain, a whistle was blown and tools were downed. Management allowed this to go

The new Crabtree press arriving in 1968

unchecked to the detriment of the paper. For example, if the press manager couldn't be bothered to wash out the trough so a new colour could be applied to an advert, the advert duly appeared in the old colour and nothing was said for fear of upsetting the union. The advertisers were left to stew in their own frustration.

However, there were little triumphs to enlighten the gloom. As all pieces of artwork had to be produced by an artist who was a union member, advertising staff kept an illicit roll of SLADE stickers tucked away in a draw which ensured the smooth passage of the ads through process.

Yet the biggest complaint of all, naturally, was pay. It was about this that tensions first boiled over into industrial action. On March 13, 1971, the 140 journalists of all the Priestgate papers withdrew their labour when offered a rise that would take them to £30-a-week. They joined a national strike called by the National Union of Journalists (NUJ) involving 9,000 provincial journalists all demanding an increase in the offer from the Newspaper Society – a 'union' for newspaper owners which negotiated national pay agreements with the trades unions on behalf of the owners.

Yorkshire Television came to Priestgate to capture the scenes of the first official journalists' strike in 101 years (the printers had had a minor spat in 1959). "Mr Evans said the paper was being produced editorially by himself and six executive journalists working as reporters during the day and sub-editors at night," reported the programme. "In addition, people were ringing in with news and old friends and old contacts were helping by supplying information, many exclusive stories resulting."

Managing director Frank Staniford said: "*The Northern Echo* has survived many difficulties throughout the past century and has not yet missed an issue, and the management is determined to preserve that record."

The dispute in Darlington seems to have fizzled out long before the official settlement date of December 21 when the Newspaper Society agreed to rises of between £5.25 and £7.25 per week – not far from the NUJ's demand for a £7 across the board rise.

This, though, was a dry run for what was to come.

In August 1976, the combined NUJ chapels in Darlington passed a resolution unilaterally declaring a closed shop. It set the union on a collision course with management who refused to entertain the notion. A couple of non-union new recruits arrived and with judicious words whispered in pubs about the merits of joining the brotherhood along with cataclysmic warnings of the consequences of not their joining, they all saw the error of their ways.

Then in April 1977 Josephine Kirk-Smith was appointed to the Darlington and Stockton Times. Educated at Cheltenham, she had previously written a column called Tots and Teens for The Lady magazine and, now divorced, was looking for a way back into journalism. But she wasn't a union member. The persuadings and the cajolings could not move her – she was even asked by the general secretary of the NUJ whether she was a Jehovah's Witness or an extreme Baptist which might have excused her membership on religious grounds. Then she decided to join the Institute of Journalists, a rival, more moderate union. The NUJ was furious.

"They thought they'd got a simple-minded female; well, I was not about to be bullied. They were looking for an argument and unfortunately they chose me as the kingpin," she told the Sunday Times.

Don Evans, the editor of WP's flagship paper, must have felt like his famous predecessor WT Stead had he looked out of a porthole on the Titanic and seen the iceberg looming.

In the upstairs room of the Red Lion, the NUJ chapel voted by about 45 votes to 37 to withdraw its labour. May 1977 saw a series of one day strikes before, on June 3, a permanent strike began.

Pickets from all over the country came to Priestgate in 1977 to support the Great Strike

The vote in the Red Lion was hardly overwhelming, but it was enough. Indeed, had pay and conditions been better, the point of principle about the closed shop wouldn't have been so important and the vote probably would have gone the other way. Yet senior reporters and subs took home about £45-a-week and after 36 years experience, the deputy chief reporter was earning £48-a-week. Although the grass is always greener in someone else's pay packet, comparable journalists in Newcastle and Middlesbrough were earning £15-a-week more and enjoying perks like company cars and shift payments. Yet management countered by saying that eight of the highest paid strikers were on £85.08-a-week and the average pay of strikers was £62.67. What is more, on a turnover of £4.09m, 48 per cent went on labour costs and North of England Newspapers pre-tax profits of £257,000 didn't allow it to pay any more.

The strikers ran off their own magazine, entitled Bulletin, to keep them entertained on the picket line and a ditty by John North perhaps best captures their feelings about the role of pay in motivating their action:
"In working days, ere magic did begin
And the name of NUJ echo with a ring
There dwelt in Priestgateland a quiet tribe
Of subs, reporters and their fellow scribes
Who observed the peace and called it freedom.

Their lot was blessed, they thought, to earn as much
As half the rate at the Gazette and such;
Mileage was ten pence, with more for tea
So what if the basic wage was penury?"

Seven junior North of England journalists found that they were better off receiving the NUJ's strike pay of £30 than they were working normally. As well as the Echo's low wages, this tells something of the commitment of the NUJ to the strike. It was desperate to take on WP in particular and the Newspaper Society, which had just set up a secret anti-closed shop fighting fund, in general. Darlington, home of the famous Echo where it happily was strong, was the ideal battleground.

The NUJ's momentum was fuelled by the fevered atmosphere of the nation – although Queen Elizabeth II's Silver Jubilee coincided with the start of the strike, more thoughts were concentrated upon the Grunwick dispute which was reaching its bloodiest – and by its argument that the only way Darlington journalists could force WP to pay them more was by using the weapon of unity through the closed shop.

This was a contradictory position to take on a newspaper which had campaigned against the closed shop at Durham County Council in 1951 on the grounds that it was an affront to personal freedom of choice. Yet the management position was equally contradictory: it had tolerated a closed shop among printers for decades but now wouldn't allow one on the journalists' floor.

The management tried for the moral highground by claiming that if all journalists had to carry a union card, the NUJ would be dictating who could be employed and so the whole concept of freedom of the press and freedom of expression was threatened.

"If management were to concede a closed shop to the NUJ we would be turning our backs on the IoJ, whose trade union rights have up to now been recognised," said managing director Bill Butler. "We fully recognise that some journalists want a closed shop for industrial purposes, but the overriding factor is the freedom of the press."

But the NUJ was willing to accept a code of conduct that somehow enshrined such freedoms. "The NUJ is not threatening the freedom of the press: it seeks only to gain the legitimate bargaining power enjoyed through the closed shop by many other workers, including printers and publishing workers of *The Northern Echo*," said the Darlington Father of the Chapel, Mike Duggan. And, as the strike unfolded, it became clear that the ultimate freedom of the press – the freedom that allowed the presses to roll in the first place – lay in the hands of the printers whose closed shop management accepted.

Amid claim and counter-claim, the Echo was reduced to an 18 page then a 14 page publication of dubious quality produced by Evans and three other executives.

Outside, the pickets organised themselves with military precision. "Darlington will be picketed Monday to Saturday, 7am to 7pm, Sunday 4pm to 7pm, and every morning from midnight until around 3am," said the Bulletin, drawing up the rota. "There are six main picket groups and each day five will be on duty for one three hour shift. Each group gets a day off in turn but faces 7am duty the day after."

At first the picketing was good-natured. "Although there are probably a couple of militants...the impression the majority gives is of reasonable men and women almost embarrassed by their action," said the Sunday Times of June 19. "It is difficult to find anywhere that spark of fanaticism needed to make a strike successful. Picketing might grow harsher in desperation, but mainly it has been uselessly polite: even Mrs Smith has received the occasional 'good morning' as she enters the office. Some pickets cannot stop themselves worrying about whether the Echo's circulation will pick up when the strike is settled."

On Friday nights, the picketline mood changed as North of England employees were augmented by NUJ activists from Glasgow, Sheffield, Newcastle and Kettering. The Scots' long journey south lubricated their grievances against the Darlington management. It became commonplace for a Friday night raid to be essayed with pickets flying into the despatch room off Priestgate's Back Lane to stop the presses rolling and the paper leaving. The police tried to prevent them, occasionally meeting violence with violence – representatives from the Council for Civil Liberties officially complained about the police behaviour and Darlington mayor, Ces Spence, said on radio that he saw an officer punch a picket. With tempers running this high, there were several injuries – one picket was severely crushed by a delivery van and a couple of press operators picked up nasty knocks trying to repel the pickets' raids. And, of course, there were arrests. Usually these were just single pickets, often not from Darlington, who had tried the police's patience too much, but on the Friday nights of June 24 and July 1 there were 15 and 25 arrests respectively. Court cases often collapsed in confusion as the NUJ's lawyers were able to expose the inadequacy of the police evidence, although many pickets were fined £10 plus £10 costs for committing public order offences.

The Friday night raids regularly reduced the print run to 30,000 copies instead of the usual 112,000 – but *The Northern Echo* was still appearing. Just. On June 6, Don Evans headlined his report on the weekend's action which almost thwarted his best efforts: "The nearest thing you ever saw – as Wellington said."

The footnote explained: "The Duke of Wellington after Waterloo said: 'It has been a damned nice thing – the nearest run thing you ever saw in your life'."

On July 22, even Wellington would have been staring defeat in the face as the dispute deepened. The TUC Printing Industry Committee ordered NGA and SLADE members "to give full and effective support" to the NUJ. This meant they would not cross the picket line; the press would not run; *The Northern Echo* would not appear.

Leon Brittan, Conservative MP for Cleveland and Whitby, called on the Labour Government to intervene because there was "a risk of an important regional newspaper closing down"; Darlington Labour MP Ted Fletcher supported his call although he also supported the strike.

The front page of Tuesday, August 1, 1977, read: "It is possible that this could be the last issue of *The Northern Echo* to be published for a while after an unbroken record of more than 107 years of continuous production.

"Until now the strike has been ineffective, all the newspapers continuing to appear by the work of executives or IoJ members, but today printers and blockmakers may join in on the instructions of their national leaders.

"This means that we will not know until tonight whether or not Wednesday's editions of *The Northern Echo* can be produced.

"If not, we apologise in advance to readers and thank them for their continuing support over the past eight weeks both in continuing to buy a depleted paper and by their letters and telephone calls of encouragement and support.

"We apologise to advertisers who will lose revenue by being unable to tell the public what they have to offer.

"We apologise especially to newsagents, many of whom rely upon *The Northern Echo* for a large part of their income, and who in times of troubles have often come to collect the papers themselves rather than see them fail to publish."

It was a very bald statement by Don Evans, shorn of sentiment or emotion. It was left to deputy editor Maurice Wedgewood to emote. His Alexander Spokesman column had taken over from John North who was picketing outside and became by far the most readable part of the strike-bound paper.

Alexander Spokesman drew long and hard on his pipe and wrote: "33,401...I mention it for the record. No 33,401 on the front page today means that the paper has been published, come hell or high water, on 33,401 days of intended publication.

"It represents 33,401 links in a chain kept unbroken through decades of storm and stress, illness and ill-hap – stretching back to a January morning when a bellman cried word of a New Daily Newspaper for the North of England, at a people's price of one halfpenny.

"It represents a promise kept, through three generations, to the people the paper is all about, the people who read it; to those people especially who say they would be 'lost without it'.

"It represents a faith kept through 33,401 harassing nights and days, with craftsmen and journalists who have put their hearts and skills into keeping that promise, sweating against the clock.

"It represents 33,401 pulse beats of a paper's life blood.

"I mention it...for the record.

"With 33,402 in mind.

"In case the pulse stops beating."

On Wednesday, August 3, 1977, the pulse stopped beating. *The Northern Echo* failed to appear for the first time in 107 years, eight months and two days. Its previous closest scrape with the unimagineable had come on October 27, 1954, when a local electricity cut left the journalists working by candlelight as the hot metal cooled. But the power had been restored just in time and the first edition left the presses 50 minutes late. Now, with no printers to run the presses, there were no editions at all.

The Northern Despatch tried to escape the shutdown by putting typewritten sheets of news in the Priestgate windows, which the sub-editors on the picket lines delighted in correcting with black felt-tip pens on the glass.

The Darlington and Stockton Times also fell silent – "it's like taking their Bible away from church", Sir Timothy Kitson, MP for Richmond, pleaded on behalf of his farming constituents to strike leaders in the Red Lion – as did the Durham Advertiser Series. A bulletin of births, deaths and marriages did come out of Priestgate, published on a photocopier by classified manager Anne Blood and telead manager Jean Adams. Up to 3,000 copies of each edition were distributed for display in newsagents' windows. It at least kept the advertising staff occupied as they had little more to do than phone their clients and plead with them to stay loyal to the Echo. As many advertising staff were commission-orientated, their pay was slashed.

As well as the BMDs bulletin, the strikers' Bulletin was also produced. Some issues were 16 pages packed with in-jokes and picket rotas.

And "the Tardis", the NGA's portable strike headquarters arrived in Lower Priestgate. "It had duffle coats and waterproofs for pickets, water carrier and Calor gas stove," reminisced John North in January 1978. "It was wired for mains electricity but a cable could not be connected – a telephone was installed and a television just in time for Boycott's one hundredth hundred."

Negotiations continued throughout the summer, autumn and winter of 1977. In December, the NGA stepped in to broker a peace deal but when the NUJ rejected its recommendations, it decided it had had enough. Blaming journalists' "intransigence" it balloted its members about a return to work. "Fury as NGA vote to go back," raged the Bulletin of Thursday, December 8, and on Tuesday, December 13, the strikers worst fears were realised when the Tardis was removed from Priestgate – pressed into service at a more winnable NGA dispute in Bristol.

On Friday, December 16, No 33,402 of *The Northern Echo* appeared. "Good morning," said the first of 16 pages. "It's great to be back. We hope you think so too."

The leader read: "*The Northern Echo* is back in circulation today after 116 lost issues. Naturally we are glad to be publishing again, and sorry for all that has been lost – by readers, by advertisers, and by *The Northern Echo*. There are losses all round, not least among people on strike.

"The paper is again being put out by its four senior editorial executives with the help of one reporter and three photographers."

There were still 100 journalists outside on the picket line and their resolution lasted until Wednesday, January 11, when they voted by 85 to five with five abstentions to return to work. The following day's Bulletin cleverly could be read either way up: "Victory. Cash now, house agreement, expenses, NUJ guarantee," said its front page. Turned upside down, it read: "Defeat. No closed shop, house agreement unlikely."

Britain's longest news strike ended with neither side victorious. The strikers had been given better expenses and allowances, the promise of better pay and temporary productivity deals in which they had to cover for departed colleagues in return for immediate money. In subsequent years, their pay levels did improve. But, after 19,612,800 seconds on the picket line, they had not won the closed shop battle.

Guy Keleny, the local NUJ press officer said it was "not what we would call an excellent settlement but it does represent a substantial gain".

The Northern Echo leader of Monday, January 16, 1978, said: "With the welcome return of more than 50 journalists to their desks all over the North-East during today, *The Northern Echo* from tomorrow can be itself again after 32 long weeks. What has happened in that time can be relegated to history, save perhaps for a word of regret that for 19 of those weeks no paper at all could be published, breaking a record of more than 107 years without the loss of a single issue.

"This has been like a long and painful illness, with its crisis and slow recovery into convalescence, receding into memory as full vigour returns."

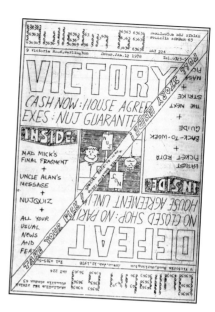

A poster showing printers and journalists united in 1977

The NUJ strikers' magazine showing the uncertain nature of the settlement

It was with vigour that the Echo set about enticing its readers back with offers of free Co-op stamps and a Mark the Ball competition which had a £790 Phillips video cassette recorder ("which tapes TV programmes", it explained to readers who didn't understand the new technology) as top prize. There was a new football column by Liverpool star Steve Heighway, and a news column by Tony Edwards based on the spoof bulletins at the start of the Two Ronnies TV show – Edwards was the show's principal writer. A new series entitled Lords of the North began looking at the lives of North-Eastern peers, and Sid Chaplin started a new series "recalling the warmth of the old pit villages".

Yet there was still unfinished business. On December 5, 1978, the local chapel of the NUJ voted 51-38 with five abstentions to strike again, demanding a 50 per cent pay rise as opposed to the Newspaper Society's offer of 8.7 per cent. The strike, a national one involving 8,500 journalists, started on December 14 but was crumbling by January 5 and on January 18 the union voted to accept a 14.5 per cent rise.

Some of those who took part in the strikes look back on them with pride, particularly in the organisation and solidarity, and joy at sticking two fingers up at a distant, disliked management that had previously appeared invincible. Some of them positively enjoyed the experience as they spent eight months with their children and decorated their homes. Others, however, express their sorrow. As the original vote showed, they didn't want to be on strike and were there only because they were "members of a club, and as such you abide by a club's rules".

And when they returned to work, there was bitterness and recrimination. One newcomer spoke of finding "deeply-soured relationships"; another said "there was an awful lot of folklore and demons left over".

But the greatest loser of all was *The Northern Echo* itself. When the "Great Strike" started, it was selling 112,572 copies day; by the end of the second strike, its sales had dropped beneath 100,000 – with a fair proportion of copies sold to people collecting the free Coop stamps. Its cover price was down to 4p but its costs, particularly journalists' wages, rose. As well as the 10,000 sales that the strike permanently deprived the Echo of, there was the lost advertising revenue. Estate agents, for example, suddenly found there was an alternative to North of England Newspapers' titles, and it took four years for all of them to be wooed from the South Durham Times.

Don Evans shortly before his retirement

Circulation down; revenue down; costs up; profit down to barely three per cent.

Just when the rocket needed a steadying figure in command, Don Evans found his personal problems multiplying. He had flirted with alcoholism during his days in Durham in the 1950s and now in the late 1970s, his habit re-emerged.

"He had enormously torn loyalties during the strike," said one senior editorial figure who witnessed the aftermath. "His heart was with the chapel; his head was with the management. The drink was one way he managed to cope with it. There were many who felt the Great Strike did for him."

It was all too much for Westminster Press. In 1980, London parachuted in a young Canadian called John Pifer from an Oxford freesheet. He landed in the upper echelons at Priestgate in a new executive position. His mission was to prop up Evans and to take on some of the more established members of staff who weren't running the paper in the way WP deemed suitable. London's especial concern was that local news was banned from the front page of the Great Daily of the North.

With such a brief, WP's bright white hope was never going to be popular. But his arrogance ensured that even those ambivalent to his appointment were quickly against him – an attitude shared throughout the building. He didn't help himself when he formed an Echo wine club – just the idea raised eyebrows among staff and Shildon readers alike who still preferred a pint to a glass of foreign stuff.

The Pifer period came to a head when Frank Peters, the chief sub from Harold Evans' day who had worked through the strikes and was now night editor, headed south for Fleet Street. On his last front page on January 16, 1982, he left a coded message in the first letter of the headlines on the column of digests down the right of the paper. The headlines, some of them stretching the story to fit the scheme, read: Freeze ending; Up and up; Child-saver; Keep out; Plane iced-up; Inflation steady; Feathered find; Everybody out; Rolling on.

The wordsearch appeared only in the first Yorkshire edition. It was spotted on the stone and pulled although, by then, Peters seems to have had a change of heart and phoned in asking for it to be changed.

To many in Priestgate, the hidden message matched their own thoughts perfectly. To others, though, it is one of the saddest days in *The Northern Echo's* history. However apt the sentiments, it is not appropriate to air dirty linen in public.

Pifer lasted only a couple of months after being exposed to ridicule by his own front page, and Evans followed soon after. His personal problems had intensified with the outbreak of the Falklands War as he had a son in submarines. "He would come back at 10pm or 11pm after having had a drink and pore over the PA copy expecting to see his son had been sunk," said a senior figure of the time.

Evans was 56 when a job was created for him as Westminster Press London Special Correspondent for evening papers. "He was told to retire," recalled the senior

The famed Pifer wordsearch

figure. "He had produced that paper for WP almost single-handedly during the Strike, and after 17 years of service, he was being treated shoddily."

Four years later, WP closed its London office. Evans became acting editor of the UK Press Gazette for three months before retiring. He died in August 1997.

The clear-out at the top in Darlington left the way clear for WP to insert another of its proteges, but rather than a memo announcing his imminent arrival, his first mention in Priestgate came in the most bizarre of fashions. On May 26, 1982, John North took offence at an article written by former Northern Despatch reporter John Lewis which appeared in a weekend freesheet called the Crawley Herald. Lewis' article began: "Darlington is a typically grubby little Northern market town." Mr North urged all Darlingtonians to write in outrage to the Crawley Herald at 12 The Boulevard, Crawley, West Sussex. They should address their disgust direct to the editor, one Allan Prosser.

In the three months before he came to *The Northern Echo* to take up the editor's position, Prosser answered several letters from enraged Darlingtonians. He told them they were being over-sensitive. But, fortunately, this was not the first time he had come across the great paper.

14 Prosser years and press tears

Allan Prosser, editor in the 1980s, managing director in the 1990s

I N 130 years that *The Northern Echo* has been attacking the devil, three editors' reigns stand out for their innovation and energy. There is the fury and fire of WT Stead's preaching; there is the nerve and drive of Harold Evans' campaigning, and then there is the vision and direction of Allan Prosser's modernising.

Prosser was just 30 when his heavy footsteps first shuddered Priestgate's shaky floors in August 1982. He'd started as a trainee reporter 12 years earlier at the Ealing Gazette and had worked his way up through Westminster Press' outer London papers. In 1977, he'd redesigned and relaunched the Acton Gazette series and in 1980 he'd performed the same task on the Crawley Observer series. For his work at Acton, he'd won a design award; for his work at Crawley, he'd won a Newspaper Society award for the weekly newspaper with the highest percentage circulation increase in the country.

But Acton is as long a way from Darlington as a weekly is from *The Northern Echo*. Prosser's experience was questioned as was the fact that he was another WP placeman up from London – staff had just had their fingers burnt by John Pifer.

However, like Harold Evans, Prosser inherited a newspaper in such a condition that any changes he made would look revolutionary in comparison to what had gone before, and, again like Evans, those working closest to him came to regard his reign as the time of their professional lives.

It was Evans who inspired Prosser to become a journalist in the first place.

"It was in the middle of the 1960s that I became aware of a newspaper called *The Northern Echo* – a title straight out of the pages of AJ Cronin, all dark satanic mills and thundering, reforming, zeal," said Prosser. " I was in my second year at grammar school, vague notions about becoming a journalist swirling around in my head. It was the era that Cassius Clay beat Sonny Liston for the world heavyweight championship; the Great Train robbers went to jail; Mods and Rockers used to scrap it out in ritual battles at seaside resorts every Bank Holiday – and I became hooked on a scratchy, black and white TV programme broadcast from Manchester called What The Papers Say.

"Its frequent presenter was a Buddy Holly look-alike called Harold Evans. What impressed me was that this eloquent advocate, based in a faraway place of which I knew little, was campaigning on a major national issue...and winning. Evans was out for nothing less than the abolition of capital punishment by focusing on the miscarriage of justice that surrounded the execution of Timothy Evans more than a dozen years earlier.

"I was intrigued. It seemed to me that if a regional newspaper dealing primarily in local news far away from the centres of power in the United Kingdom could make such a difference then this was a profession worth pursuing.

"The years passed. I went through journalism college and, as luck would have it, the publishing company I joined owned *The Northern Echo*. Almost from the first day I was determined to become its editor. But, as with most ambition, it made sense to keep such thoughts to myself."

When the job came up, he didn't take much persuading. "On a pre-decision reconnaissance we drove overnight from London and breakfasted on cheese sandwiches and strong coffee watching the sun rise over Gunnerside. The decision to move North was made in a moment," he said.

"In the winter of that year *The Northern Echo* could not be described as 'a happy ship'. It had not recovered from a debilitating strike that had deeply soured relationships; circulation was dropping consistently; there was a lack of productive capacity; a previous executive had departed amidst considerable acrimony.

"Most of all it was a newspaper looking back to its past. The ghosts of former editors – Reggie Gray, Harold Evans and his successor Don – stared down from the walls. Evans, Evans and Prosser, said someone, sounded more like a Welsh front row than a roll call of editors. All the best stories about what the newspaper had achieved were rooted in the 1960s."

He began tearing up trees. *The Northern Echo* became a tabloid within a broadsheet. The storycount rose; no lead should be longer than 12 paragraphs; there was more local news on the front and inside due to the editionising policy.

"Although it sounds beguilingly simple now, we resolved to implement a number of consistent policies," he said. With beguiling simplicity, he then listed them:

"1. The paper would carry more local and regional news, mainly through the mechanism of increased editionising. Within four years the amount of news covered by the paper increased five-fold." At its height, there were seven editions and, as the newspaper as a whole became more business aware for the first time since the Starmer era, adverts were also editionised.

Prosser's list continued: "2. Local and regional news would fight for its space on page one and, when it was compelling enough, we would lead on it.

"3. The paper's reputation for provocative, campaigning, and uncomfortable journalism would be rekindled. There would be major coverage of important events – the miner's strike; the attempt to locate nuclear waste at Billingham; the Cleveland Child Abuse crisis; the peril of AIDS-contaminated blood."

The Miner's Bible's rather sat on the fence during the miners' strike of 1984 but from there it assailed both sides. "Arthur Scargill looks destined to join that band of tragic, heroic figures whose unfailing optimism blinded them to the fact that even as they were proclaiming imminent victory they were in reality half way down the Swanee," said a leader in January.

In March: "The future of mining can be assured: its decline must certainly be arrested. But this will not happen while miners continue to be treated with contempt by Mrs Thatcher, Mr MacGregor (Ian, chairman of the National Coal Board), the leader they elected for life and smug commentators who neither know, care about nor share their problems." In tired desperation, deputy editor and leader writer David Flintham invented a Mr MacScargill character whom the paper urged for the good of both sides should take a long holiday.

The Cleveland Child Abuse Inquiry, which investigated claims that doctors using controversial techniques had diagnosed that children had been abused by their parents and took 121 of them into care in five months, saw *The Northern Echo* report the inquiry in vast detail for its entire four-and-a-half months. For the three days that the prime witnesses, Drs Marietta Higgs and Geoffrey Wyatt, were at the stand their evidence was reported verbatim, taken down in shorthand by two reporters.

Princess Anne gives Allan Prosser the 1988 Regional Newspaper of the Year Award

That in itself did not come cheap. "More money was invested in journalism than for many years," said Prosser. "People began to take notice again. Journalists were attracted to *The Northern Echo* because they had a chance to do their job properly. Award followed award.

"The paper, once again, became a consistent design award winner, placing those trophies alongside those it held for content. On one memorable occasion (1988) it was named the UK Press Gazette's first ever Regional Newspaper of the Year at Birmingham's NEC. A local Midlands evening paper had booked a suite and put the champagne on ice so confident were they of victory. The Echo's team celebrated with pints of beer instead."

Prosser's list of simple tasks continued: "4. Technology would be totally overhauled. We would move into the computer age. No longer would anyone would be able to ask the question put during Local Newspaper Week in 1984.

"Visitor: 'Do you have Caxton's original printing press in here?'

"Editor (looking puzzled): 'No. Err, why?'

"Visitor (smirking): 'Because you seem to have all the rest of his equipment.'

"During the period 1984-1990, *The Northern Echo* became one of the first papers in Britain to introduce computer-based graphics and to archive its content electronically into searchable databases."

The electronic library of 1987 was indeed very advanced for its day, although the print unions were still able to demand that the new-fangled graphics be dismantled so that they could re-set every word the graphics contained. Similarly, in terms of computer typesetting and on-screen page make-up the Echo was 20 years behind foreign newspapers, even those in Africa, and was one of the last regional newspapers in Britain to make the switch from hot metal to bromide. Still, by 1989, no one in Priestgate had recourse to touch a typewriter ever again.

Anne Blood, advertising manager in the 1970s

But Prosser's tasks still weren't complete: "5. Cover prices would be held. Conventional marketing wisdom at the time was that newspapers were relatively price-insensitive. All the sales figures told us otherwise. A premium pricing policy was not going to be effective in a region where train works, mines, steel plants and manufacturing industry were closing every week.

"And it certainly wasn't effective in the 1990s when Rupert Murdoch started his price war, or 'pricing promotion' as News International preferred to call it.

"6. Finally, more effort would be invested in staff relations. The 1980s was characterised by the tensions which accompany periods of profound industrial change and we had our share of brush fires. But, despite pressures to the contrary, and alone among the titles owned by the parent company, we resisted suggestions that we should derecognise the unions. We preferred to demonstrate that there was merit in making good agreements, and keeping them. In this, as in other areas, *The Northern Echo* was ahead of its time as the decade closed."

That, then, was how *The Northern Echo* was transformed during the 1980s. However, North of England Newspapers as a whole had two major problems to address, and the solving of both was to have profound implications on the Echo in the decade to come.

Firstly, there was the Northern Despatch to consider which, since March 3, 1969, had been known as the Evening Despatch and which, since 1973, had appeared as a tabloid serving Darlington and South West Durham. It had won its fair share of awards – design in 1955, 1956, 1957 and 1965 – and had got its fair share of scoops: most notably in June 1938 when the Reverend Robert Anderson Jardine disappeared from his church, St Paul's, in Northgate, Darlington, and re-emerged at a chateau in Tours, France, where he married Edward, the abdicated king, and Mrs Simpson, his American divorcee.

Yet the Despatch had long had its problems and had long had its critics. Questions about its viability were raised when it turned tabloid and, at the start of the Great Strike when it sold 16,783, Don Evans warned: "It is very much easier to stop a newspaper than it is to start it up again and gain the same level of sales as previously. If the Evening Despatch were to be stopped, for instance, it would possible it would not appear again."

The Despatch did stop, and it did appear again, but now the writing was on the window – just as its wall posters had been during the strike.

In the aftermath of the Great Strike, the company blitzed the area in an attempt to regain lost sale. The Despatch increased its circulation by 13 per cent – the biggest rise in the country in 1978 – but this was largely due to all promotional efforts being concentrated upon it to the detriment of the Echo. The blitz continued with the short-lived Echo Advertiser which ran until 1980. This paper adhered to the American concept of blanket or saturation coverage and every home in South West Durham which didn't take the Echo received the Echo Advertiser free-of-charge. It consisted of tasters from *The Northern Echo* and adverts, and it so hugely undermined the Despatch that it was clinging to life by its fingertips while its owners dug at the cliff beneath it.

Born in wartime to provide a 24-hour news service in tandem with the Echo, the Despatch was losing the circulation battle and, unlike successful city evening newspapers, it had no major football club to feed off. Advertisers did not want to know.

"It should have closed after the Second World War," said Anne Blood who was advertising manager at the time. "The only reason the Despatch stayed open for so long was because Bill Butler, the managing director, fought for it because so many people depended upon it for their livelihoods.

"There wasn't a market for it and we were being forced to sell adverts into it at £4 a centimetre whereas the competitive frees in the area were charging 60p a centimetre. The Despatch didn't generate enough advertising revenue nor cover price revenue to support a full journalistic staff. The South Durham Times was knocking everything in sight. We weren't competing – you don't need so many journalists or production staff to produce a series of frees."

The Despatch's fingerhold was prised from the cliff face by the 1986 report by McKinsey management consultants. They advised scrapping it and the assorted weeklies (apart from the Darlington and Stockton Times) in the stable and replacing them with a comprehensive series of free Advertisers to saturate the area and wipe out the competition.

There was some opposition to the McKinsey plan at the highest levels in Priestgate which at one point almost led to the mass defection of the advertising staff who were contemplating mortgaging their houses and starting their own saturation series of Advertisers.

But the decision was made. On April 18, 1986, the Despatch died.

Its death left the Echo stronger in commercial terms. However, it presented it with a new set of problems. "The Echo was rightly concerned about competition coming into the town and it ended up a hybrid of a local paper in South Durham and a regional paper elsewhere," said Peter Sands, assistant editor at the time. "Like Harold Evans, I believe that the Echo can only survive as a regional paper. Darlington can't sustain a local paper – the Despatch was circulating about 14,000 when it closed – but when the recession came it concentrated on the local and began to lose its regional feel."

That editorial debate has been rumbling ever since, and the Despatch's closure also left the Echo with a another long-running legacy. The main capital expenditure of a publishing business is on its press. It therefore makes commercial sense to have that press working as often as possible. That is why in nearly all other publishing centres a morning paper is produced on the same

Late 1980s news conference chaired by Allan Prosser (back to camera). Left to right: Peter Sands, assistant editor; David Kelly, deputy editor; Angus Goodfellow, deputy chief sub; Andy Brown, chief sub; Rachael Campey, news editor

press as an evening. The two work hand-in-hand, one paper being the main revenue earner and the other ensuring the press is still making a modest profit in the quieter period of the day.

The McKinsey plan nodded in agreement at this theory. It suggested, perhaps half-heartedly, that a Sunday Echo would be a good idea. It foresaw the opening of shops on a Sunday which could provide additional advertising revenue and it predicted the explosion of interest in Saturday sport, especially football. It also observed the weaknesses of the Sunday Echo's only regional competitior – the Newcastle-based Sunday Sun which utilises the press when the Newcastle Journal (morning) and Newcastle Chronicle (evening) aren't being produced.

But the Sunday Echo never materialised. Nor did Prosser's suggestion of a tabloid Evening Echo. Instead, *The Northern Echo* was left alone in Priestgate, with only the weeklies to support it. It was alone as its competitors radically increased their pagination, colour and magazine inserts. It was alone and being printed on presses whose origins could be traced back to 1948.

For a while, Darlington kept up the appearance of seeking to bring a new press to the town even though, with the Echo all alone, the project didn't have financial viability. In the mid-1980s, North of England Newspapers acquired the site of the Peases' woollen mill in Crown Street and imagined what it would be like to site a state-of-the-art press there. An entire office of advertising, journalists and production staff could be built around it, allowing Priestgate Palace to be relinquished to the developers who were eyeing up Darlington town centre as a suitable shopping centre.

However, presumably because of the potential for the property scheme, in 1987 the company changed tack. It applied for planning permission to build a new press hall in Enterprise House, formerly the home of the engineering company William Press Ltd, in Valley Street, Darlington. General manager Vernon Lester told the council that if the plan were refused, all printing would be transferred to York with the loss of 50 jobs. As any reporter knows who has had the good fortune to sit through council planning meetings, the threat of job losses is a good way to plough your plans through, and the council passed the application. It also granted Westminster Press outline planning permission to build a shopping centre on the Priestgate Mill site.

WP was beaten to the tills, though, by the Cornmill shopping centre which sprung up a few yards away in the heart of Darlington's town centre. For the rest of the century, life in Priestgate was punctuated by a regular flow of rumours that Starmer's old building was on the verge of being sold to the Cornmill. Negotiations have been nearly as regular as the rumours, particularly in the

The Crabtree Viscount MkII press in operation in Priestgate: "an ugly engineering solution who served the Echo well".

early 1990s, but the "golden key" proved elusive.

WP was probably as serious about becoming a shopping centre owner as it was about building a new press in Darlington. In London, Darlington's problems were easily combined with another WP division at York. Darlington had one morning paper plus some weeklies and an old press. York had a small evening paper plus some weeklies and an old press. Why spend £8m on two brand new presses just 50 miles apart when £4m on one press was all that was needed?

The question then was where to locate that one press.

"The decision to share print resources was sound," said Prosser. "Big assets such as presses have to be worked 24 hours each day. But the print centre should

Emergency packers in 1992: sub-editor Ken Farrier, senior systems assistant Dave Frankland, deputy editor Rachael Campey, assistant editor Terry Murden, works overseer Cliff Howe

have been established as a separate company, probably on the A1 close to Wetherby. From here it could have serviced York and Darlington and provided spare capacity for major cities such as Leeds and Bradford. It could have competed for national business. But it was not to be."

Blood also favoured the sharing of the print resources. "I have always thought that presses are penis extensions for some men!" she said. "All I wanted to do was sell advertising and sell papers." She, though, suggested that somewhere off the A19 would have been appropriate.

Yet York had a canny trick up its sleeve. It argued, quite correctly, that traffic poses a major hazard in the historic city centre. It is almost continuously on the verge of grid-lock. An evening paper – which has a far shorter post-print life than a morning which may be printed at 3am but not required for sale before breakfast – couldn't make it to the city centre newsagents if it were printed outside the ancient lanes. Therefore, concluded York, any press printing the Yorkshire Evening Press must be within York city centre.

Now hang on a minute, replied Darlington. If newspapers, which are generally small enough to slip through letter boxes and only need little vans to deliver them to newsagents, can't get into York's crowded streets, how are huge articulated lorries bearing vast reels of newsprint going to reach the city centre press? Surely, concluded Darlington, it would be better to print outside York, allowing the vans to wend their way through the traffic and keeping the artics out.

No, no, no, replied York. Newsprint doesn't have to come by road alone. It can come up the River Ouse and into the Fosseway canal by barge. Conveniently enough, York's city centre headquarters in Walmgate had its own landing stage where the barge could moor.

York won the day. The press was built there. But its argument was specious. In 1996, Newsquest bought Westminster Press and asked the new managing director of York, Anne Blood, why it was costing £100,000 a year to bring newsprint in by barge. Looking at the figures, Blood was unable to come up with a justification. Indeed, in the face of environmental protests about adding to the heavy haulage in the historic city centre, she found that lorries bringing in newsprint would add just 0.0012 per cent to York's congestion. There had been no need all along to base the press in York city centre.

Of course, the argument about the location of the press could just be seen as petty rivalry between two divisions who felt they were being dragged up the aisle into an arranged marriage by their parent company, WP. And of course the argument would have had no import whatsoever if the press had worked properly wherever it had been located.

"We wanted to be able to produce two backset tabloids every day and we wanted 16 pages of colour every day," said Blood. "That's what we were told we would get."

It didn't happen. The £3.5m new press was French, a Rockwell Visa. It was the first of its kind in the country and only the second of its kind anywhere in the world. It was still a prototype.

Its specifications seem to have been drawn up somewhere in London. When it arrived in York in early 1990, the head of the installation crew is supposed to have denied all knowledge of a regional morning newspaper being printed on his equipment. Then he had to increase its capacity by 60 per cent.

But, on June 30, 1990, the Darlington presses were formally decommissioned. After 120 years of printing silenced only by the Great Strike and by those two wartime Tuesdays when the Durham exercise was tried, Priestgate's nights were no longer alive to the sound of hundreds of tons of metal creating a newspaper.

"I was familiar with the press' sound, its smell and its minders," recalled David Kelly, then managing editor. "I had been there on many occasions – though mostly to get a chisel taken to a plate when a literal had been spotted.

"On that final night – or so we believed it to be – I climbed up to the gantry with sub-editor Sue Kendrew, who had hurried back from holiday to be there, as the last plates for first edition were being locked into place.

"A klaxon would sound each time the press was crawled to allow a plate to be positioned and, that night, the siren seemed to wail from its heart. It is, of course, completely silly to believe a machine – an engineering solution – has a soul. But that is how it seemed then.

"When the press was started, the crew quickly adjusted the inking and then the speed was increased. Though I was watching all this and the rev counter, soaking it in, my abiding memory is of the vibration that spread up from the gantry through my body. The press was possessing us for the last time.

"When it was finally racing, I confess my eyes were watering. And the crew? I'm sure a number of them were so focused on getting it right that they could keep the emotion hidden in those inky overalls.

"It was a night full of melancholy. The smell of paper, ink, machinery. Ink stains on your hands. The taste of tears.

"She was an ugly old 'engineering solution' who had served us well. Little did any of us imagine the nightmare that was to follow."

The Northern Echo was now one of only three papers in the world produced digitally using on-the-run colour – pages made up on a site remote from the press and transmitted to it in digital form and printed in colour all in one go. Gradually, its printers were retrained or made redundant, and its 1948 Hoe Crabtree press was dismantled leaving only the 1968 Viscount Crabtree.

Fortunately, there was still life in the Viscount. Ten times in 1990, the Rockwell Visa failed to produce a paper and the Viscount was pressed into action. During 1991, as editions were dropped and colour became smeared, the Rockwell became more reliable but still had its moments of madness. "It was the first day of the football season and it wouldn't work and we had to condense a 48–page paper into a 24-page which was all the Darlington press could manage," said Sands, now editor. "There was even talk of dropping the sports section!"

Then came April 10, 1992. The press refused to start altogether. To make matters worse, this was General Election night.

"I got a phone call at 10.30pm from the managing editor David Kelly," remembered Blood, by now managing director. "I had just got out of the bath. I was told there was an electronic fault and they couldn't start the press. I got to the office and had all the pages laid out on the floor and ultimately decided that we had to take all the ads out and leave all the news in."

Desperate phone calls were made to Bradford to see if its press could be used, and to old-timers in Darlington who knew how Viscount Crabtree worked. Early in the morning, it spluttered into life and reeled off about 7,000 copies.

"But we had no despatch department," said Blood. "We had to make a chute out of two ladders with some canvas across them just to get the papers out of the press room.

"There were many times that press had me in tears of frustration. We finished getting the papers out at 8am and we were filthy dirty and then I burst into tears."

York, though, had miraculously come to life again and the full print run was completed – but not in time for breakfast.

"Our election coverage had gone superbly well," said Sands. "We had 41 constituencies with graphics on each of them and by last edition we had a graphic of how the nation had changed and a very comprehensive coverage. Then I saw David Kelly standing at the edge of the subs room and I knew there was a problem.

"It was heartbreaking. We went to the Golden Cock for breakfast and I left at 8.30am and went across the road to the newsagents and asked for an Echo. They just laughed. The Evening Gazette was already there. All our energies and resources and three months of planning – gone.

"I got a letter from a reader who said he had had some friends staying with him and they'd wanted to stay up to watch the election unfold but he told them not to because *The Northern Echo* would be delivered in the morning with it all in. But his paper hadn't arrived and he was very disappointed. I wrote back

Princess Alexandra starts the Rockwell Visa Press in York in 1990

saying I understood exactly how he felt and asked him how he thought I felt?"

Blood resolved that the election fiasco would never happen again. "I got in touch with a scrap merchant and told him to come and take a torch to our press," she said. "While there was a parachute, York would be happy to let us use it."

Perhaps this drastic action focused minds in York. Although the Echo has come perilously close to not appearing since then, York has always managed to get some sort of a paper out. But right into the late 1990s, it was not on time. It arrived in Darlington long after shiftworkers were in the factory and long after the paperboys and girls had gone to school. Editions were dropped, almost at random. News local to one area appeared in another. Colour reproduction ranged from muddy to smeared. Readers cancelled; advertisers fumed.

"No one knows who carried the can for the press – if anyone," said Blood. "It only came with one colour satellite and Darlington had to justify the £1m cost for another one.

"From day one, that press has never given Darlington a fighting chance to meet its marketplace."

Said Prosser: "The press at Walmgate was under-specified to give Darlington the production flexibility it required for its portfolio of titles and products; colour reproduction was inconsistent. Worst of all print times suffered, jeopardising and then turning back the sales advances of the previous seven years. It was dismal and demoralising – and, above all, distracting – time for all involved, especially as it coincided with mounting pressure for increased profitability."

Since 1998, the Rockwell Visa has, by and large, behaved itself. This may be put down to it finally bedding in, to the crews finally becoming accustomed to its wiles and to the various extra attachments increasing its capacity.

Yet all is not well that ends well. The press is still too small for the needs of a regional morning paper like *The Northern Echo*. Whereas its competitors are awash with colour, the Echo gets it front and back with odd slots on pages 3 and 9. Whereas as its competitors are awash with pages and supplements and sections, the maximum the Echo can produce is 48 broadsheet pages. Primarily because of the lack of colour, as much as £100,000 of advertising a year is being turned away, and however brilliant the stories and the design, the Echo struggles to provide sufficient value to entice readers away from its tightly-packed competitors.

The 32-week long Great Strike of 1977 is estimated to have lost *The Northern Echo* 10,000 in circulation; the decade-long saga of the York press is believed to have done even greater damage.

15 Owners and editors

I N ONE decade, *The Northern Echo* had five editors, four managing directors and three owners. The only constant was the problems with the press – although there was also a perpetual maelstrom of rumours and speculation about the next twist that the tempestuous 1990s were going to take.

The period of incessant change began in May 1990 when Bill Butler retired after 15 years as managing director of North of England Newspapers. He was succeeded by Anne Blood, the marketing manager.

On Christmas Eve in the same year, editor Allan Prosser left to take up a new post with the Kent Messenger group. "Editing a morning paper for seven volatile years was physically taxing," he said. "I had young children who were born to us at Darlington Memorial Hospital (and who still delight in telling their Southern friends that they're really Northerners). It has also always been my view that editors should get out before they have to be pushed."

The editor's chair was taken by Peter Sands. A North Shields lad whose love of Newcastle United FC was as profound as Prosser's of Chelsea, Sands had joined the Echo in 1979 as a sub-editor. After chief sub-editing the Evening Despatch shortly before it closed, he had worked his way up from night editor.

"It was a dream come true for me," he said. "It was hard, though, because the paper wasn't in its cups, but there was still a lot to do. I wanted to retrieve its regional status and the new technology was allowing us to go into new publications: Echoes, which was aimed at older readers, and 7Days, the entertainments magazine, both added value to the paper."

Prosser and Kelly had taken the paper into the colour era and Sands redesigned it so that, in 1991, it again won the National Design Award. "We increased staff quite considerably and initially it was very, very good," he said. "The paper was driving along."

Yet after colour's initial euphoria, the press problems began to drain the editor's resolve. He wrote to York complaining about the "cavalier fashion" in which the paper was being treated. He termed it "the vandalism of *The Northern Echo*" and the fiasco of the 1992 General Election was "a catalyst in my career".

"Some days, I could take no pride in how the paper looked and it would be a lie to say that that didn't have a bearing on my leaving," he said.

He also had worries about the future. Pearson, the parent company of Westminster Press, was coming under sustained criticism from market analysts for the disparate nature of its empire, certain corners of which were not making profit enough to prop up its new found interests in computer software and television. Whereas Prosser had managed to peg the paper's price at 18p since 1985, Sands' three years saw it rise to 30p. "It was practically a 2p rise every nine months," he said. "Accountants told me that every 2p meant an immediate loss of 2,000 on the sale. Although you usually clawed that back, it became difficult to sustain a growth in sales."

In 1993, Darlington was making 12.5 per cent profit – a record. But other newspaper groups like Thomson and Northcliffe were returning 20 per cent. WP began fiddling with its operating culture, changing lines of communication. The "pod" system of grouping reporters, photographers and sub-editors was beginning to evolve. "Some of it was valid, but it was motivated by the bottom line," said Sands. "There were redundancies in the offing which I was uncomfortable with. We were drawing back from the developments like the supplements and there was pressure to close offices in Sunderland, Newcastle and York which we needed if we were going to be a regional newspaper."

Having glimpsed the future, and witnessed the unhappy effect his long hours were having on his three young children – "my wife was effectively a single parent family" – he called it a day and became director of the WP Editorial Centre in Hastings.

August 1993 heralded the return of former deputy editor David Flintham, this time as editor. Since leaving Darlington in 1986, he had edited the Bath Chronicle and the York Evening Press. *The Northern Echo* was a logical career move, especially as he had aspirations to become WP's editorial director. He said he wasn't employed to take on senior staff as rumour had it, but instead set about tackling what he saw as the contradictions at the heart of the paper.

"In Darlington it was a local paper, an Evening Despatch," he said. "Elsewhere it was a regional in a region that didn't exist: North Yorkshire, for example, wasn't really that interested in County Durham. We retrenched into our heartland where the paper could provide a regional coverage and a local service.

"Its news agenda was rather elitist, relying on diary stories and breaking news which it did brilliantly. But you couldn't rely on breaking news so you had to build up stories and look at topics that really mattered to people." 'Think like a reader' became his catchphrase, and he developed the relationship between editorial and newspaper sales. "While newspapers have to have a spirit," he said, "they also have to sell copies."

Soon Flintham was back in tandem with his old editor Prosser. In 1994, Blood became advertising director for all WP and Prosser was lured to return as managing director of both York and Darlington. Like Sands, both of them had seen the future – although neither of them realised how vicious it would be.

Managing directors in the 1990s: Anne Blood, Allan Prosser, David Kelly

In April 1995, with North of England Newspapers making 15 per cent profit on turnover, the demeanour of WP changed. Out went Hew Stephenson, part of the old paternalist regime, and in came a young thrusting chief executive called Stephen Hill. His orders were simple. "He was told to get WP ready for sale," said Blood.

His methods were ruthless. They had to be. WP was not making enough to justify its existence as a cash cow to bankroll Pearson's new "info-tainment" projects.

Although Prosser warned darkly about the future, the reality did not hit home in Darlington until he returned from a meeting with the new chief executive. "Allan called department heads together and opened the meeting by saying 'shit happens'," said Flintham. "He'd been told WP wanted 20 per cent profit margin by the end of the year and if the managing directors couldn't do it, Stephen Hill would find people who could."

A cost-cutting plan was compiled, Prosser adding a chapter on the likely consequences of such rapid actions. Suddenly he found WP was talking about separating his empire into its constituent parts of York and Darlington.

"It was obvious that *The Northern Echo's* parent company was having its margins fattened for sale," he said. "A new chief executive was brought in to ginger things up. He had scant interest in the medium or long-term impact of his decisions on the fine newspapers that had served Muker and Middleton One Row, Toft Hill and Tudhoe for more than a century.

"It was time to explain that to him; then it was time to go."

He went to develop his career on the internet – "a medium of infinite possibility, just as those newspapers launched in the second half of the 19th

Century must have seemed to the Victorians". In a crisis, Blood was called back as managing director and she had a little more time for Hill's plans. "He was 85 per cent right," she said although, like Prosser, had little success in convincing Hill that *The Northern Echo*, a paid-for regional morning paper, was commercially different from a free, weekly advertising paper.

In June 1995, 51 redundancies were announced at North of England Newspapers – a cut of about an eighth of its staff. At the time, a £7m rise in the cost of newsprint in the previous eight months was blamed and although this was a contributory factor, others saw less honourable motives.

"Fifty-one people are being sacrificed for corporate greed and the quality of these highly-profitable newspapers will suffer," said the local NUJ.

"It was awful, absolutely awful," said Blood.

"It was very distressing," said Flintham. "I had a reputation for cutting staff numbers as I had done so at Bath and the York Evening Press, but there I was able to give myself a noble motive in that by moving money around I could use it better and improve editorial.

"But this time it had nothing to do with editorial or ensuring the future prosperity of the paper. If it had been losing money, I would have been able to justify it to myself and others."

From Pearson's perspective, however, the tactic worked. Westminster Press' profits for the first half of 1996 soared to £16.2m compared to £4.2m in the first half of 1995. The group was now ripe for sale, although when its sale was completed its new owners said they had bought a company suffering from low staff morale.

Harold Evans in the newsroom in November 1998

Flintham's temperament was no exception. He was not necessarily the jolliest of people in the best of times and those around him saw him at a low ebb.

As Prosser had predicted, the cuts bit deep into the paper's circulation and when allied to the continuing, debilitating press problems, *The Northern Echo* was in the process of losing daily sales of 20,000 in seven years. For Flintham, the prospect of the editorial director's job was also gone, the post being another victim of the cuts.

"Having worked extremely hard for three years I could see a lot of it being wasted, and there was no promotion to look forward to," he said. "Nobody would have been happy if they cared about the paper. I wasn't going to sit there and give the impression that everything was hunky dory."

His disposition was not improved by discovering that shortly before the redundancies were announced, North of England Newspapers was about to launch an Investors in People programme on the edict of WP. Then he found himself and his staff forced to undergo a personal development programme entitled Winning Edge.

"It was an absurd semi-psychological programme designed to put a deceitful gloss on increasingly serious problems and it seemed to me to be symptomatic of the times," he said. "In terms of what was happening and the resources we were putting into the paper, I found it very difficult to deal with because I believe in being at least as honest as it is wise to be."

He left in August 1996, shortly before Pearson closed the deal which sold WP to Newsquest, a company formed in 1995 by a £205m management buy-out of the Reed group's 120 local newspapers.

Backed by the US venture capitalists Kohlberg Kravis Roberts and the UK media investment fund CINven, Newsquest had been forced to up its bid for WP at the last minute from £295m to £305m because of intense competition from Independent Newspapers of Ireland and United News and Media. This, though, was short of £350m that Pearson had hoped for.

Newsquest's chief executive was Jim Brown, a 61-year-old Scot who had started out as a junior reporter on the Ayrshire Post and whose career had advanced so that now, with the addition of WP's 62 titles, he was in charge of one of the three largest media companies in the country.

He was in a position to take stock of the cuts pushed through in the dogdays of WP which, according to the Daily Telegraph in September 1997, WP "insiders" described as "indiscriminate" and "potentially damaging". Brown told the Telegraph that Hill had had a "big job to pull this business out of the mire" and had done a "lot of things that should have been done years before". However, the Telegraph summed up Brown's analysis of WP by saying he had found his new titles suffering from "low staff morale, inadequate investment in marketing and overly aggressive cover price increases".

The Northern Echo's predicament went further: not only was it without an editor but Blood had ended her 25 year connection with the paper in June by becoming md at York. She now watches developments from not-so-afar as md of Northeast Press at Sunderland.

Her replacement was ready-made – general manager Kelly, who'd been with the paper since 1976 when he arrived as Features Editor, stepped up – but finding a new editor was not so easy. For eight months editorial was run by deputy editor Peter Barron. Editing the Echo was a job he desperately wanted. He had joined in 1984 as a reporter having told Prosser how he'd been sacked as racing tipster at the Scunthorpe Evening Telegraph for backing too many losers. He'd followed the newsdesk route to become Flintham's deputy, and now hoped he was onto a winner. He threw himself into Saving the Bishops – the Bishop Auckland football club was in danger of going out of business but *The Northern Echo* rallied the local community and the illustrious Manchester United to save the day. But for Barron, this time around at least, there was no storybook ending. Andrew Smith from the Bolton Evening News was appointed.

"It's like finding out that the man who's been sleeping with your wife is actually a very nice person," said Barron having met Smith and in November he reluctantly departed to edit the Hartlepool Mail as he had been told that a candidate for the editor's chair in Priestgate ought to have had experience editing elsewhere first.

Smith himself had been editor of the Mail between 1987-92 and came to Darlington from the Bolton Evening News, a Newsquest title. A Tynesider whose only spell outside the North-East in his 27 year career had been his five years in Bolton, Smith was fully aware of *The Northern Echo's* history and reputation.

"I would crawl up the A1 over broken glass to edit *The Northern Echo*," he told Kelly.

Smith explained why: "I started in 1970 as a trainee reporter and then sports editor on the Blyth News which was part of Westminster Press. *The Northern Echo* was our regional morning paper and we had to phone over major news stories from Blyth, like the closure of the Northumberland pits of Fenwick and Nedderton, and football reports from the Spartans. It was quite something to get a story in *The Northern Echo* – and to be paid lineage for it."

But he didn't find the paper at its healthiest in February 1997. "Its circulation was awful," he said. "It was losing four or five per cent sales a year and I had to reduce that decline without additional resources – when I left, the decline was less than two per cent. Having worked for Newsquest for five years, I was aware

Editors in the 1990s: Peter Sands, David Flintham, Andrew Smith

of how it drove its business – it didn't throw money at editorial.

"I saw the Echo as a regional morning newspaper. It can't survive in its current form as a local for Darlington or South West Durham as the area isn't big enough to support it commercially.

"I felt it had been to the detriment of the paper that it had closed its office in Newcastle, the regional capital, and one of my successful objectives was moving an extra reporter into North Durham to cover Tyneside.

"I felt that to be a regional paper, it was understaffed. When Harold Evans visited in 1998, he said he didn't know how I ran the paper with a staff of 66: in his day there had been over 110 journalists. He said he would go back to New York and tell his friend Henry Kravis that we were understaffed." Kravis was head of the KKR group of financiers which bankrolled Newsquest.

Smith was in charge for two years which produced two momentous news stories. On May 1, 1997, Tony Blair, the leader of the Labour Party and MP for Sedgefield in the paper's heartland, won the General Election by a landslide. "It was a great night simply because we were the organ that could deliver local results first in the most comprehensive way with comment and interviews from all those involved," said Smith. "Ten North-East MPs went straight into government and the paper gained even more influence."

Then on August 31, Diana, Princess of Wales died in a car crash in Paris – "the biggest story of my career and one of the biggest this century outside the world wars". The mood in the office was "electrifying". "The adrenaline was flowing throughout the newspaper all week and we did a great job covering the story properly on a national and regional level," he said. "It culminated in me being invited to the funeral as the representative of the people of the North-East and that was a huge accolade for *The Northern Echo*."

It also culminated in *The Northern Echo* publishing for the first time in its 128 years on a Sunday at the end of one of the most extraordinary weeks in modern British history. The 24 page Sunday special, including Smith's report from inside Westminster Abbey, was as good – and probably better – than anything any national newspaper published.

"The journalists wanted to do it and the management were fully supportive regardless of cost and logic," said Smith.

In the immediate aftermath, on the suggestion of Barron, Smith picked up on a campaign he had rejected earlier: to raise £¹/₂m to complete the Butterwick Children's Hospice in Stockton, the only children's hospice in the North-East. "I'd rejected it because I didn't think the impetus was there to raise that total in an acceptable period of time, but when we said we were doing it in memory of the Princess of Wales the result was spontaneous – within nine months we had the total."

Once that campaign was concluded, Smith began to have doubts about the future.

"Newsquest was heavily supported by American financiers who saw their investment as a five-year return and there were already rumours that they wanted to capitalise on their investment," he said. He dreaded the prospect of another financial house buying the company "and squeezing it for another five year term – I didn't feel the paper could take any more redundancies if it wasn't going to be fundamentally damaged".

His apprehensions coincided with an approach from Northeast Press in Sunderland to become its editorial director. The group included his first paper, the Hartlepool Mail and the Sunderland Echo, which he was asked to edit.

"I had met Peter Sands while working my notice at Bolton and he'd said that from the day you become editor of *The Northern Echo* start to plan your exit because there are no editorships in regional papers bigger or better than *The Northern Echo*," said Smith. "I was concerned personally about what would happen to me if I survived the full five or seven-year term. The Northeast Press offer came three years too soon and I left the Echo job half done but for

Doug McCorkindale, president of Gannet, with Jim Brown, Chairman of Newsquest

personal and family reasons and for long term prospects it was too good to refuse."

He left in January 1999 and the way was open for Barron to return, now experienced enough to lead *The Northern Echo* in to the 21st Century after his 13 month sojourn in Hartlepool. "I see the paper as trying to be something for everyone," he said. "It's a local paper for Darlington and South West Durham, a regional paper for the North-East and North Yorkshire and a national paper as well. It has to have a balance of all three."

However, almost as soon as Barron arrived, Smith's soothsaying proved right and the tempestuous 1990s dealt *The Northern Echo* another radical change. Quietly, in March 1999, Newsquest was put up for sale. The group's operating profit of £63m in 1997 had been more than three times 1996's £20.7m. In 1998, it had improved by 29 per cent to £81m and in June 1999 the American media giant Gannett offered £904m for it.

Gannett can trace its roots back to the summer of 1864 – when the Darlington Establishment was barely aware of the maverick Henry King Spark who catapulted it into starting *The Northern Echo*. Printer James Reynolds was travelling to California when he stumbled across the town of Boise, Idaho, where the 1,000 residents were crying out for a local newspaper. He started the Idaho Statesman in a log hut, and went no further.

That title still exists and was one of those acquired by Frank E Gannett who started his empire in 1906 when he bought a half interest in the Elmira Gazette in Elmira, New York State. At the time of its acquisition of Newsquest, Gannett, based in Arlington, Virginia, boasted the largest group circulation in the US. It owned 74 daily newspapers including USA Today, and 21 television stations.

At the dawn of the 21st Century, *The Northern Echo* was a very profitable enterprise: in 1999, it was two or three times as successfully financially as it had been six short years earlier.

It was also dabbling its toes in the waters of the media of the new century through its thisisthenortheast website, and it hoped that the last, global, twist of the traumatic 1990s could provide the stability to which it had been accustomed for much of its 130 year history. Above all, it hoped that its press would continue to behave itself until a replacement could be acquired.

But, away from the tales of how Frank E Gannett as a nine-year-old in Rochester, New York State, started his first paper round delivering the Democrat and Chronicle, of how at the tender age of 12 he started employing friends to collect the skeletons of dead animals to sell to a fertiliser firm,

Peter Barron: editor 1999

and of how at as a 17-year-old student in 1892 he sold news stories for $1 a time to The Buffalo News of Bolivar, there were still devils to be attacked in downtown Darlington.

Barron was schooled in the Prosser academy of campaigning journalism where he was joint winner of the North-East Journalist of the Year for his part in securing a £20m trust fund as compensation for the families of 12,000 haemophiliacs whose loved ones had been infected by Aids. On June 1, 1999, he found himself caught up in a tragedy very close to home.

The Northern Echo's deputy chief photographer Ian Weir died from a heart attack having waited seven months to see a consultant about a heart by-pass operation. He was 38.

To Weir's distressed colleagues, his untimely death summed up much that was wrong with the National Health Service. After years of under-investment, the new Labour Government was committed to cutting waiting lists – all waiting lists. There was egalitarian merit to this approach, but the NHS was lagging behind the rest of Europe in its treatment of its most acute cases. Government policy meant that those patients with potentially fatal conditions, like Weir, were being treated in the same way as those with less serious problems.

It was wrong. After much deliberation, the Chance to Live campaign was launched aimed at getting the Government to change its waiting list policy so that treatment times for those with cardiac complaints could be decreased to nearer the European standard of three months.

The first sign of success came in the summer of 1999 when the Conservative Opposition, led by Richmond MP William Hague, changed its policy so that the most serious conditions would be given priority. Mr Hague cited *The Northern Echo's* campaign as a direct influence on his "common sense policy".

Opportunely, in the Cabinet reshuffle of October 1999, Prime Minister Blair, who was himself aware of the campaign being one of *The Northern Echo's* MPs, made Darlington MP Alan Milburn Secretary of State for Health. Within seven days of being office, Milburn, also citing the Chance to Live campaign, had summoned the country's cardiac specialists to Whitehall and announced that life-threatening conditions like heart problems and cancer would be given priority treatment. He also set in motion a six-year plan to bring Britain's coronary care treatment in line with the rest of the Continent.

Barron summed up the victory in an internal memo. He said: "It is no exaggeration to say that we have gone a long way towards changing Government policy as well as redefining Tory Party policy. Although resources will never be enough, £50m for 3,000 extra heart bypass operations is a solid enough beginning."

Kelly's memo said: "A compelling argument, marshalled and managed to great effect. And what higher reward can there be than to save people's lives?

"This campaign was in the finest traditions of *The Northern Echo*."

After 130 years, *The Northern Echo* is still attacking the devil – and beating it.

Acknowledgements

T O start where I usually do at the Darlington Centre for Local Studies, my thanks go to the staff there: Kimberley Bennett, Brian Myers, Margaret White, Katherine Williamson and Gillan Wilson. Maurice Wedgewood, the former deputy editor who died shortly before this book was completed, did much of the spadework.

My thanks to colleagues in the Features Department and the editor Peter Barron who carried me through; to Jane Whitfield in *The Northern Echo* library; to photographers who copied pictures with nary a moan; to Echo Memories readers who constantly fed snippets and to Paul Gliddon and Karen Conlon who fed theses.

I would also like to thank all the former editors and executives, especially Harold Evans and Allan Prosser, who were generous with their time, candid with their opinions and rewarding with their gossip. To the Red Lion for providing inspiration and my computer for not losing a word.

A mention too for Andrew White, Phil Ward, Phil Robson, Steve Wetton and Greg Marshall; a particular mention for Colin Tapping who is still promising to buy the beer and read the proofs, and for Richard Simpson who painstakingly laid out those proofs; and a special mention for David Kelly for his enthusiasm, his attention to detail and his financial backing which allowed me to indulge myself.

And finally to my wife Petra and my baby daughter Genevieve who were lulled to sleep every night for many months by my midnight tapping at the keyboard and were then bored to sleep every following morning as I relived every word.

My sincere thanks to one and all.

Bibliography

Newspapers of Northumberland and Durham by Maurice Milne (Northumberland Press, 1971)

The Westminster Press Provincial Newspapers by AP Duncum (Westminster Press, 1952)

Darlington Newspapers by John Robert Page (Darlington Corporation, 1972)

North of England Newspapers: Decline in Political Influence 1900–39 by Paul Giddon (unpublished thesis 1999, University of Newcastle)

The Book of Darlington by George Flynn (Barracuda Books, 1987)

Memories of Darlington I by Chris Lloyd (*The Northern Echo*, 1993)

Durham at the Opening of the 20th Century by J Jamieson (WT Pike and Co, 1906)

My Father by Estelle Stead (Thomas Nelson, undated)

The Life of WT Stead by John Kensit (unpublished, undated)

WT Stead: Saint or Sensationalist by Victor Pierre Jones (Gooday Publishing, 1988)

WT Stead: Campaigning Journalist by Karen Conlon (unpublished thesis, 1984, Newcastle Polytechnic)

Durham 13 by WT Stead (*The Northern Echo*, 1874)

Almost 50 Years of *The Northern Echo* (*The Northern Echo*, 1917)

The Great North Country Newspaper (*The Northern Echo*, 1928)

British Political History: Democracy and Decline 1867–1990 by Malcolm Pearce and Geoffrey Stewart (Routledge, 1992)

An Editor's Faith by L Worstenholm (Wm Dresser and Sons, 1937)

Memories of George Gilbert Armstrong, Journalist, Politician, Author, Preacher, Apologia pro Vita Sua by GG Armstrong (1944)

Editing and Design Book 5: Newspaper Design by Harold Evans (Heinemann, 1973)

A History of Gannett, 1906–1993 by J Donald Brandt (Gannet Co. Inc., 1993)

Archives of *The Northern Echo*, the Darlington and Stockton Times, the Northern Despatch, the North Star, the Darlington Mercury, the Darlington Telegraph and the Darlington Pamphlet

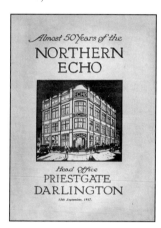